D1447491

THE CHEMISTRY OF DEATH

Publication Number 544

AMERICAN LECTURE SERIES®

A Monograph in

AMERICAN LECTURES IN LIVING CHEMISTRY

Edited by

I. NEWTON KUGELMASS, M.D., Ph.D., Sc.D.

Consultant to the Departments of Health and Hospitals
New York, New York

THE
CHEMISTRY OF DEATH

By

W. E. D. EVANS, M.D., B.S.

Senior Lecturer in Morbid Anatomy
Charing Cross Medical School
University of London
Honorary Consultant in Pathology
Charing Cross Hospital
London, England

CHARLES C THOMAS • PUBLISHER
Springfield • Illinois • U.S.A.

Published and Distributed Throughout the World by
CHARLES C THOMAS • PUBLISHER
BANNERSTONE HOUSE
301-327 East Lawrence Avenue, Springfield, Illinois, U.S.A.

© *1963,* by CHARLES C THOMAS • PUBLISHER
Library of Congress Catalog Card Number: 63-11520

*With THOMAS BOOKS careful attention is given to all details of
manufacturing and design. It is the Publisher's desire to present books
that are satisfactory as to their physical qualities and artistic possibilities
and appropriate for their particular use. THOMAS BOOKS will be true
to those laws of quality that assure a good name and good will.*

Printed in the United States of America
V-1

FOREWORD

Our Living Chemistry Series was conceived by Editor and Publisher to advance the newer knowledge of chemical medicine in the cause of clinical practice. The interdependence of chemistry and medicine is so great that physicians are turning to chemistry, and chemists to medicine in order to understand the underlying basis of life processes in health and disease. Once chemical truths, proofs and convictions become sound foundations for clinical phenomena, key hybrid investigators clarify the bewildering panorama of biochemical progress for application in everyday practice, stimulation of experimental research, and extension of postgraduate instruction. Each of our monographs thus unravels the chemical mechanisms and clinical management of many diseases that have remained relatively static in the minds of medical men for three thousand years. Our new Series is charged with the *nisus élan* of chemical wisdom, supreme in choice of international authors, optimal in standards of chemical scholarship, provocative in imagination for experimental research, comprehensive in discussions of scientific medicine, and authoritative in chemical perspective of human disorders.

Dr. Evans of London discusses the process of dying and the nature of somatic death as great clinical disguisers and inevitable chemical adventures; the exterior signs of death from loss of movement to rigor mortis due to stretching of muscle threads that lost ATP; the spontaneous and artificial postmortem changes from the earliest alterations in tissues to those found in very ancient specimens; the chemical changes associated with infarction of various tissues during life; the application of chemical findings to the assessment of the time of death and the dating of old remains; the real causes of complete cessation of functional and metabolic activities; the development of adipocere and its relationship to mummification; and the final conversion of the body by air, water, and earth to its fundamental elements in the light of the author's extensive experience.

Death to the physicist is irreversible non-functioning; to the biologist, the tension between termination and fulfill-ment; to the theologian, the moment of life's termination; to the physician, the final stage in the dynamics of life. Death is really part of our self, manifest in the genes of the ovum, and functioning within our tissues and blood more actively before birth and during infancy than in youth and maturity. Growth and death are the resultants of irreversible chemical changes taking place progressively within the tissues and blood, the substratum of physiological time which slows down from infancy to old age. Life opposes its own progress but gradually yields to the forces of disintegration, the vital price exacted for compactness of body and agility of move-ment.

We are so accustomed to think of death as the fate of all living things, that we forget that protoplasm is immortal; all life springs from pre-existing life. The flame is handed from torch to torch, the torch extinguished, but the flame con-tinues to glow. How did death arise? Is it inherent in life? It is obvious that the individual who would live alone shall surely die but for all others Nature perpetuates indi-viduality in the gallery of family portraits. The family line is represented by the germ plasm and the individual mem-bers, by the somatoplasm. Death has thus been evolved for the good of the race, not the individual, to remove the de-bilitated in favor of the vigorous. The de-building principle parallels the creative at every moment of man's existence; his life is in fact a series of little deaths. The fever called living is conquered soon enough but death remains the servant of life which can attain mastery over death.

We can distinguish the disintegration of the unity of a living being and the interruption of the interrelationships with tissues, blood, and consciousness and with the external environment as instantaneous, delayed, interrupted, or protracted death. The body remains almost entirely alive after death is definitive. Organs and tissues begin to die, each in their turn. The tripod of life formed by the heart, lungs, and brain may be overturned irreversibly but independently. When the heart stops, the liver continues to make glucose, the muscle still responds to stimulation, the hair reveals growth. Just as there may be local death in a living body, so there may be local life in a dead body. The possibility of life recovery is thus a wholly artificial sign of death. There appears no sharp demarcation between seemingly dead tissue, whose life has flickered to a smouldering ember, fanned back into flame; and the handful of dust, the aggregate of of compounds into which the decomposing body finally crumbles, with the material returned to the inorganic world for newly formed life.

The codified necropsies of Morgagni give us an insight into the nature of morbid death; the classical works of Brouardel, into sudden death; the experimental studies of Carrel, into physiological death; the chemical investigation of the author, into somatic death. The ancient concept of death was expressed in the image of Parcae who carried a scythe to cut the thread of life. Modern thanatology considers exitus the precondition to life in existentionalism. All life processes lead to structuralization whose irreversibility deceases life potential and thus increases entropy. Death sets in when life has fulfilled its transformation of the unstructured into the structured, hence man's age is not measured by distance from conception but from death. It is a question of how long can he live rather than how long has he lived, and the amount of structuralization possible applies to the total organism as to the single cell. The age of the cell is not measured in terms of the number of past cell divisions but by the carrier capacity of the total destiny of the organism. Medical science is just beginning to conquer from the riddle of life in the abyss of the body, the mystery of death. But, we shall never outwit Nature, we shall all die as usual. Mortem effugere nemo potest.

"With what strift and pains we come into the world we remember not; but 'tis commonly found no easy matter to get out of it."

I. NEWTON KUGELMASS, M.D., PH.D., SC.D., *Editor*

INTRODUCTION

Living and dying are processes, transient it is true, but dynamic, with many episodic fluctuations which tip the balance first this way and then that in an unending challenge to medical skill; whereas death, the absence of life, is no more than an irreversible, static and unvarying state of little or no intrinsic interest. Such is the picture so often formed by the undergraduate medical student to whom death, so far as materialistic concepts go, is apt to appear both figuratively and factually as the end.

Nothing could be further from the truth.

Death is not an unaltering state, and far from being an inert mass, the dead body is, under normal circumstances, subject to many complex and, often enough, only partly investigated changes arising from intrinsic as well as extrinsic causes which bring about quite substantial chemical and morphological alterations of the tissues, though attention has tended to be drawn more to the visible structural modifications than to the chemical changes.

While direct and microscopic observations of dead tissues provide a good deal of information, it is becoming increasingly recognized that the investigation of dead tissues requires further and more subtle approaches, such as those of general biology, bacteriology, virology and serology, and chemistry. It might be thought that these sciences are already fully utilized in modern postmortem techniques, but in fact they are far more commonly employed only in attempts to infer the antemortem conditions which had been present in the tissues themselves rather than to investigate postmortem changes proper. In other words, the tests have tended towards the "clinical pathology" of the dead; though all too often without the necessary normal controls relating to dead tissues. For this reason the results of some of the various specialized tests on dead tissues must be viewed with some dubiety, as the possible disturbing effects of postmortem changes may not be known with certainty.

The importance of increasing the knowledge of details of postmortem changes is brought out particularly in the investigation of deaths where specific morphological changes are minimal or unhelpful—the "functional" deaths—which are by no means always found to be due to poisoning by extrinsic agents: assessment of the time of death, too, calls for an understanding of tissue changes after death which, all too frequently, is sufficiently defective for the calculations to be little more than inspired guesswork guided by collateral circumstances.

This is not to imply that no work has been done on postmortem changes, because a number of aspects of the topic have been closely investigated, ranging from those bearing upon the storage of edible meat, when early postmortem changes are of great importance, to the more remote fields of archaeology which are providing information on the effects of long postmortem intervals on tissues. The gaps in knowledge are, however, numerous and great and it would seem that the time has come for these deficiences to be tackled, for myths and fancies of the past to be exploded, and for the study of postmortem changes to be put on a proper modern academic level. Only thus may a reliable foundation be laid upon which to base confident rather than speculative conclusions about antemortem conditions deduced from dead tissues. Not the least part of such a study is chemical investigation—the chemistry of death.

ACKNOWLEDGMENTS

Invaluable practical help in the study of post-mortem changes has been given me over the years by technicians at Charing Cross Medical School, and it is a pleasure particularly to thank Mr. H. Oakley, whose untiring assistance at numerous exhumations and autopsies has been of the greatest value, Messrs. F. Humberstone and K. James whose laboratory skills have overcome endless difficult technical problems, and Mr. K. Turnbull whose expertise has preserved many a valuable specimen. The Clinical Research subcommittee of Charing Cross Hospital has provided generous grants at various times which have enabled research to be pursued in some of the aspects of postmortem change.

Mr. B. Armitage and his Staff in the Medical School library have patiently sought and found many papers and books for me, some of them old, obscure or rare, and I am especially grateful for their unfailing courtesy in bringing to my notice any literature which might otherwise have been passed by.

Considerable help has always been forthcoming from Doctor J. Swale, also of the Medical School, to whom the author has never turned in vain for elucidation of the experimental and theoretical aspects of many chemical problems.

Many thanks are also due to Mrs. Anne Collier who has succeeded in producing an orderly typewritten text from an almost incomprehensible manuscript.

In their various ways the foregoing helpers have contributed to this book, but none can be held responsible for errors and omissions; for all these the author alone must take the blame.

W. E. D. E.

CONTENTS

THE CHEMISTRY OF DEATH

Chapter One

POSTMORTEM CHANGES IN GENERAL

PUTREFACTION

U NDER natural conditions an initially intact body commences to decompose immediately after death, unless modifying factors such as extreme cold or a dehydrating environment operate. The very earliest phases of decomposition are at the cellular level and are not evident grossly, but gradually the more obvious changes develop: the cornea clouds over, the body begins to cool and rigor mortis makes its appearance. Haemolysis commences and discolouration of the tissues heralds the production of gases. In time the body swells, many of its tissues soften and the characteristic odour of putrefaction obtrudes. The destructive process continues with liquefaction and disintegration until eventually the remains consist of little more than the harder resistant tissues of bone and teeth, cartilage, lens, hair and nail.

Putrefaction is a visibly active process which proceeds at a much faster rate than the other forms of spontaneous postmortem change, and the physical alterations which occur, rapidly and radically alter the gross appearance of the remains. Impressed by these changes, Bacon (I) explained them as the work of unquiet Spirits of Bodies which, wishing for release, break into confused and inordinate motion in a struggle for freedom, their activities producing putrefaction—a view now to be accepted with some reserve.

SOME BIOLOGICAL FACTORS

Putrefaction is characterized by the progressive break-down of soft tissues and the alteration of their protein, car-bohyhdrate and fat constituents: it is due essentially to the actions of many enzymes, some of which are already present in an active or a latent form in the tissues, while others are derived from micro-organisms and fungi such as Penicillium and Aspergillus, and, sometimes, from insects which may be mature or in a larval stage.

Shortly after death, organisms from the intestines migrate into the local tissues and gain access to lymphatics, blood-capillaries and veins, and thence by way of tissue planes and the blood and lymph, to the body tissues generally. In many instances a similar bacterial invasion commences from the respiratory system. Aerobic organisms deplete the tissues of oxygen and, although their numbers are reduced as the available oxygen diminishes, they create favorable chemical conditions for the more destructive anaerobic organisms which are derived mostly from the intestinal canal, though in the later stages of decomposition some may be from soil or from the air. The bacterial flora thus changes from the aerobic groups, exemplified by the coliform-staphylococcal-proteus varieties, to the anaerobic in which the Clostridia predominate.

The growth of fungi is fairly commonly found on decomposing remains, filaments and colonies becoming visible on the skin and exposed surfaces, and, as a later event in some cases, in the intestines and body cavities. Fungal growth is enhanced by a lower relative humidity than that favoured by bacteria, and the increasing acidity of tissues tends to inhibit the development of bacteria more than that of fungi and yeasts. Most of the fungi encountered upon decomposing remains are aerobic, consequently their growth is restricted to surfaces and little deep penetration of tissues takes place: for the same reason the activities of fungi are slowed and arrested in the reducing conditions which occur in sealed coffins.

The influence of fungi upon the decomposition of tissues is said to have been the basis of the tests applied to the soils of Baghdad by the 9th Century physician Rhazes, when he was selecting the most suitable site for a new hospital. Fresh meat was applied to the soils of different localities and the rate of decomposition noted. The differing rates of decay of the test meat have been ascribed to the varying concentrations of Penicillium in the soil (Golin).

Insect larvae which may cause focal liquefaction by proteolysis include species of Lucilia, Calliphora, Musca and Piophila. Some larvae have remarkably specific proteolytic chemical systems, thus the larvae of Lucilia can secrete a collagenase (Hobson) which dissolves the usually very-resistant collagen, and Tineola larvae are able to attack keratin by reducing its S-S bond to —SH (Powning et al.).

Although necrophagous animals (especially those in the soil) are attracted to a dead body, they are very largely repelled during the more active phases of decomposition: they re-appear in the subsequent phases, when a great range of animals may be found attacking the now-liquefying remains. A list of such creatures from protozoa to many of the Insecta is given by Kuhnelt (I). This same author also notes (Kuhnelt [II]) that the attraction of buried bodies to Collembola is such that these insects have been discovered at a depth of 2 metres in graveyards despite the fact that normally the depth to which these insects burrow does not much exceed 10cm.

CHANGES IN FAT: HYDROLYSIS

Neutral fat is hydrolysed to some extent by intrinsic tissue lipases and the reaction commences probably within minutes after the death of the fat cells. Hydrolysis due to the intrinsic lipases proceeds very slowly and it is a relatively slight change: the activity of this particular enzyme system soon diminishes. Paper chromatographic analyses of post-mortem subcutaneous fat have shown that oleic, palmitic and stearic acids are detected by the 8th hour after death, and that while the palmitic acid increases in quantity, the oleic acid becomes more and more hydrolysed and thereby reduced in amount (Fallani *et al.*).

More extensive hydrolysis of fat is effected by bacterial enzymes, particularly those of the Clostridia (Mant 1957) although other organisms also add their quota of lipolytic enzymes. A mixture of free fatty acids is produced which increases while the amount of neutral fat is reduced.

Water is essential for this change and there is sufficient water in the fatty tissues themselves for the reaction to be initiated: thereafter, in ordinary circumstances, the water necessary for the continuation of hydrolysis is drawn by diffusion from adjacent tissues. Provided that a sufficiency of enzymes and water is available, the hydrolytic breakdown of fat continues until little or no neutral fat remains, and a mass of fatty acids marks the site of the original adipose tissue. If no other chemical change occurs, these fatty acids remain as adipocere (see page 40).

CHANGES IN FAT: OXIDATION

Fat is altered also by oxidation, which may be brought about by the action of bacteria, fungi and atmospheric oxygen. The latter, which can operate upon sterile as well as on contaminated tissues, is accelerated by visible and ultraviolet light, consequently extensive exposure of fatty tissues hastens their breakdown.

Oxidative changes in the fat are usually overshadowed by hydrolytic changes when remains are continuously exposed to reducing conditions such as occur in closed coffins in a steady state, the oxidation soon being brought to a halt. When conditions favour oxidation, fatty acids are rapidly oxidised, and a high concentration of unsaturated fatty acids (which may have been produced by the earlier postmortem hydrolysis of neutral fat) can thus result in the local accumulation of aldehydes and ketones as the oxidation proceeds. Such a reaction is known to occur when unsaturated fatty acids were abundant in adipose tissue during life, a feature of commercial importance in the meat trade because this postmortem oxidative change can lead to an undesirable degree of rancidity in the fat: prevention is achieved by regulating the feeding of the animals in the days immediately before slaughter so that the concentration of unsaturated fatty acids is reduced.

The colour of fat is altered during the usual course of decomposition, the original yellow hue sometimes fading to a whitish grey as the carotinoid pigments are bleached, while on other occasions the fat becomes a darker yellow colour when highly unsaturated fatty acids are formed. The altering fat may be tinted by the absorption of any pigments which are locally available, and secondary darkening may thus ensue. Most frequently the extraneous pigment is derived from haemoglobin and its breakdown products, and pink, red or blue shades appear in the fat: in the abdominal regions where sulph-haemoglobin abounds after death, the fat becomes greenish.

CHANGES IN PROTEIN

Protein is broken down by the actions of enzymes after death, but postmortem proteolysis does not proceed at a uniform rate throughout the body, and in general the proteins of neuronal and epithelial tissues are destroyed early in decomposition. Those epithelia which in life are anatomically related to high concentrations of proteolytic enzymes are the first to be affected after death; the gastro-intestinal tract soon loses its lining membrane, and in some cases of slow death this particular disintegrative change may commence during the agonal period. The pancreatic epithelium also vanishes quickly. Epidermis is more resistant to decomposition and it survives for a longer period, though it, too, is eventually destroyed and shed.

Proteolysis is found in the non-stromal tissues of organs fairly soon after death and it rapidly becomes a feature in the kidneys and the liver.

Most of the stromal connective tissues are scarcely affected during the earliest postmortem period, and some survive through the later phases of generalised decomposition with little change. Reticulin resists breakdown for some time, while collagen usually survives for a longer period than the other soft tissues. The firm stroma of cartilage is scarcely altered during decomposition (though its cells undergo postmortem change), but ultimately much of the hyaline stroma is liquefied, leaving in the case of fibro-cartilage the strands of collagen fairly well defined.

The onset of the postmortem decomposition of muscle protein is usually evidenced by the cessation of rigor mortis (see page 30); rigor cannot occur after the decomposition of muscle.

The rate at which proteolysis proceeds depends chiefly upon the amount of moisture which is present, the temperature of the remains and upon bacterial action. Moisture favours decay while rapid drying will retard the change to a marked degree. Proteolysis is slowed by cooling and increased by warming, provided that neither desiccation nor charring occurs, and in this respect "warming" is taken to include any process which prevents or reduces the natural postmortem loss of heat from the body, as well as any actual increase in the temperature of the remains. A warm ambient and a terminal pyrexia both hasten decomposition, and when the pyrexia was caused by septicaemia, a not uncommon terminal event, the bacteria already widespread in the tissues before death further accelerate the postmortem changes.

In general terms proteins are broken down to proteoses, peptones, polypeptides and amino-acids, and it is noteworthy that this simplification of protein provides a nutrient substrate which admirably suits bacterial growth so that the numbers of organisms increase progressively during the active phases of putrefaction, and their dispersion throughout the body is facilitated by the increasingly fluid state of the tissues.

Phenolic substances, skatole and indole, are formed by the continuing proteolysis, and gases are also evolved. At first this gaseous production is most evident in the intestines from decomposition of their contents, carbohydrates as well as proteins playing a part in the generation of gas, and the intestines become distended by carbon dioxide and hydrogen sulphide, together with some ammonia and methane.

CHANGES IN CARBOHYDRATES

The carbohydrates in the tissues are also broken down. In the earlier stages sugars are formed from glycogen, especially in the liver, and then further destruction proceeds by way of lactic acid to carbon dioxide and water, the process being hastened by micro-organisms.

THE PRODUCTION OF GASES

Mixtures of gases, generally similar to those found after death in the intestines, begin to appear in the soft tissues, imparting to them a crepitant feel until larger accumulations of gas disrupt the tissues. Blisters develop in the skin as portions of softened and partly-detached epidermis are blown out. Deeper tissues separate along fascial planes, dissected by gaseous pressure and liquefaction, and organs assume a "honeycombed" appearance. The body swells, and blues, reds and dark greens tint the skin. Discoloured natural fluids and liquefied tissues are made frothy by gas and some exude from the natural orifices, forced out by the increasing pressure in the body cavities. The eyes bulge and the tongue protrudes; skin blisters burst and the bloated trunk disrupts. Little wonder that Bacon was convinced that purposeful dynamic "spirits" wrought this awful change, and that some sects have believed that putrefaction meant "death pangs" to the deceased, and therefore that any shortening of the period of putrefaction conferred greater comfort to the departing soul.

Some authorities used to think it necessary to pack sticks of charcoal round the coffins in vaults before closing the chambers for any length of time, in order that the supposed vast volumes of "noxious, inflammable and explosive" gases generated by the decomposing bodies might be absorbed and an explosive catastrophe averted. It was a popular notion that coffins bulged and then burst open because of the pressure of the gases, and legend has it that the body of Queen Elizabeth I so swelled up that it burst the coffin with a loud crack (*Lancet*, 1957).

In the mid-nineteenth century Lewis examined coffins in vaults in London in order to see how much truth lay in these beliefs. He discovered that coffins were by no means gastight, even though leaden shells were employed (see page 51) and he found neither burst coffins nor evidence of explosive mixtures of gases. Lewis further noted that putrefaction proceeded much more rapidly when bodies lay in wooden coffins than in leaden shells, a finding which he explained on the basis of the freer access of air to the bodies surrounded only by wood.

From personal observations of many coffins in vaults it seems clear that rotting and crumbling of the coffin wood is by no means uncommon. This leads to all stages of collapse of the coffins, but these are clearly destructive changes of slow evolution and there has never been seen anything to suggest that any coffins had been violently or explosively burst open.

POSTMORTEM LUMINESCENCE

It was observed in antiquity that dead fish and meat could appear to glow with a pale light, and the wonder and fear that this must have brought to primitive man observing the phenomenon in the darkness of night or the gloom of a cave can well be imagined. Old stories, often re-told, linger on in oral tradition telling of the glowing of exhumed human remains, the awe-inspiring sight sometimes being accompanied by equally mysterious events such as the tolling of invisible bells and the calling of ghostly voices.

These fearful concomitants to the exposure of entombed or buried bodies seem to have become unfashionable in recent years; perhaps modern times have made mankind too familiar with death, and by scientific pathways have come sophistication and disenchantment. At all events, the luminescence of remains is now to be explained by natural, rather than supernatural, history.

Luminescence of dead animal remains is most commonly due to contamination by luminous bacteria such as Photobacterium fischeri, the light emanating from the organisms and not from reactions in the decomposing tissues. The organisms swarm over the remains and give light, particularly while the temperature is in the range of 15° to 30°C. (Airth et al.).

A number of luminous fungi are known, of which the commonest in Britain is Armillaria mellea (Ramsbottom). This fungus grows upon wood, and the young mycelia can exhibit luminescence which is seen at its best during the growth phase on damp wood. Wood itself has no luminous powers, and although the enquiring Bacon noted that Sallow, Willow, Ash and Hasle may become "shining" woods (Bacon VII), it is highly probable that the various woods were parasitised by a fungus such as Armillaria mellea.

In some species of luminous fungi both the mycelium and the fruiting bodies may give light (Airth et al.). The optimum temperature range for the luminescence of these fungi is within that given for luminous bacteria, and in both these cases oxygen is essential for the production of the glow.

It is possible that the luminescence which has been described of some exhumations may have been due to the damp coffin wood having a luminous fungus growing upon it and glowing in the presence of air, though this has not personally been observed at exhumations, nor indeed has luminescence of human remains from any cause. The reducing conditions normal in burials and entombments would inhibit the production of bioluminescence, and, if exhumation were delayed for any considerable length of time, the survival of the appropriate fungi and bacteria would become very unlikely.

Chapter Two

POSTMORTEM ENZYMAL CHANGES

Aｌｔｅｒａｔｉｏｎｓ in the activities of intracellular enzymes during postmortem change have only relatively recently been investigated, and a review of the effects of autolysis on cellular enzymes by Rosenholtz *et al.* shows that the majority of the discoveries have been made since 1955. The activities of these enzymes may be studied in homogenates of tissue and, by histochemical methods, in thin sections of tissues for microscopy.

Tissues for the experimental study of very early postmortem changes may be prepared in two ways: in one the vascularity of the tissue is abruptly and severely reduced, commonly by the ligation of an end-artery, so that ischaemia and anoxia rapidly lead to localised necrosis (Jennings *et al.*); in the other, excised tissue is allowed to decompose either *in vitro* under controlled conditions of temperature and humidity (Kent), or else *in vivo* in the body of the animal from which the excision was made (Berenbom *et al.*).

At first sight there might not seem to be a great difference between the necrotic tissue of an infarct and necrotic tissue maintained *in vitro* at body temperature, due allowance being made for the fact that infarction may be accompanied by pyrexia: but the infarct engenders an inflammatory reaction around its edge, and this may introduce alterations of its chemical features which are quite lacking in the isolated tissue. Obviously, too, the detailed enzymal changes found

13

in isolated cells and tissues autolysing *in vitro* may not wholly indicate the alterations which occur in similar cells remaining in their normal site in an intact living or dead body, in which the complex variables of temperature gradients, diffusion, and biological contamination may be operating.

MITOCHONDRIAL CHANGES AND AUTOLYSIS

An early visible change in the injured cell is alteration of the mitochondria: this is generally regarded as an indication of cellular degeneration, and thus of a potentially reversible state. The precise nature of "simple" degeneration is now regarded as being far from settled, for it is quite possible that some of the changes ascribed to degeneration, a vital process, may be in reality the early changes of autolysis, a postmortem phenomenon.

Ageing (and probably dying) mitochondria become swollen, and at this stage alterations in oxidative phosphorylation accompanied by loss of adenosine triphosphate from the mitochondria have been demonstrated (Ernster *et al.*), and similar changes have been found in the very early stages of autolysis (Gallagher *et al.;* Dawkins *et al.*).

More general cellular enzymal changes occur as the process of autolysis advances. Of the various enzymes studied in autolysing cells so far, two main groups can be recognized: in one are those whose activities fall off rapidly, and in the other those whose activities are reduced only slightly in the early stages. The former group includes succinic dehydrogenase (Rudolph *et al.;* Gavan *et al.;* Kent; Kent *et al.*) and cytochrome oxidase (Burstone *et al.;* Gavan *et al.;* Berenbom *et al.*), for the activities of these enzymes in heart, liver and kidney tissues decline swiftly and fall to zero by twenty-four to thirty-six hours of autolysis. In rabbit cerebellar tissues, a rapid reduction in the activity of phosphofructokinase has also been found, occurring in the first two hours of autolysis (Smith *et al.*).

In contrast, there is a much slower diminution of the

activity of acid and alkaline phosphatases, and of esterase: these activities fall off noticeably from the time at which karyorrhexis is complete and karyolysis has begun (Gossner), but the activities of these enzymes continue to be detectable for at least forty-eight hours after the onset of autolysis. Other similarly persistent activities are those of β-glucuronidase and L-leucylglycine peptidase in liver (Berenbom), and lactic dehydrogenase, malic dehydrogenase, glutamic dehydrogenase and hexokinase in rabbit cerebellum (Smith et al.).

Just how far these findings reflect the intimate changes which occur in the decomposing cell is a matter for speculation, as the exact distribution of various enzymes and their co-enzymes in the substance of the cell cannot be regarded as definitely settled.

LYSOSOMES AND POSTMORTEM CHANGES

In 1955, the concept of the lysosome was introduced by de Duve et al. (cited by Becker et al.), who suggested that many enzymes are present in high concentration in these organelles. Among the enzymes believed to be in the lysosomes are acid phosphatase and β-glucuronidase, and these substances have been used as convenient indicators in the study of lysosomes. Hydrolytic enzymes are included in the impressive content of these organelles, and as the release of such enzymes could be expected to play an important role in postmortem cellular breakdown, it would seem that the lysosomes are a constant potential threat to the integrity of the living cell: if this be true, then the break-up of lysosomes at death, perhaps by the rupture or dissolution of their enveloping lipoprotein membrane, may bring about the changes generally regarded, so far, as marking the onset of autolysis.

Just as morphological changes have been seen in the mitochondria of dying and recently dead cells, so changes in the size and number of lysosomes have been recorded in the cells from renal infarcts and necrotic livers (Becker *et al.*).

Together with the concept of the lysosome may be considered the proposition that at least some of the intracellular enzymes exist in "bound" and "free" forms, and that dissolution of the lysosome would result in the release of enzymes hitherto in the bound state. When determinations of the activities of acid phosphatase and β-glucuronidase were made in respect of bound and free forms of these enzymes, van Lanker *et al.* noted that although in conformity with the findings of others the total activities were little reduced during early autolysis, there was in fact a significant and rapid rise in the free forms of the substances and a coincident decrease in the bound forms.

The factors which bring the loss of integrity of the lysosomes have not yet been suggested, and it is clear that much work must be done before the problem of the changes of the enzyme systems within dead cells can be regarded as solved. If the lysosome theory is correct, then elucidation of the mechanisms which bring about destruction of the mitochondria and the lysosomes may provide a fundamental contribution to the understanding of death and the early, irreversible, postmortem changes.

NEURONAL ENZYMAL CHANGES

Detailed studies have been made of the visible alterations in the neuronal lysosomes of the brains of rats, the changes having been brought about either by the actions of postmortem autolysis or by antemortem anoxia, with or without a degree of cerebral ischaemia (Becker *et al.*). The effects of autolysis were followed in halved brains from animals not deprived of oxygen, the non-autolysed halves serving as controls. The tissues were fixed in ice-cold formol-calcium.

Ordinary histological staining methods confirmed the rapid loss of intracellular details in the autolysing cells, all the details being lost after twenty-four hours, by which time the cells were homogeneous. The first change in acid phosphatase activity was seen in ten minutes, and the lysosomes, normally 0.3 to 0.7 μ diameter, became swollen and often clumped and they were reduced in number in ten to sixty minutes. After this time there was a progressive loss of lysosomes until by eight hours, most of these structures had vanished.

Similar findings were obtained from the freshly-examined brains of rats after the animals had been made anoxic by exposure to nitrogen atmospheres, and in the brains of further rats in which some cerebral ischaemia had been produced by ligation of one carotid artery before exposure to the nitrogen.

Becker and his co-workers drew attention to the capability of the many enzymes known to exist in neuronal lysosomes of destroying cell constituents, and they suggest that, amongst the reactions brought about, the release of ribonuclease may well cause disruption of chromatin.

A most important practical consideration which arises from the findings of these experiments is that unless a brain is suitably fixed immediately after death, or the autolytic changes significantly retarded by rapid freezing, little reliance can be placed on the results of histological and chemical investigations of the cellular changes which had occurred before death. This difficulty is one of the major problems in the search for indicators of anoxia in human tissues obtained postmortem (see page 26).

ENZYME LOSS FROM NECROTIC TISSUES

The progressive distintegration of dead cells is accompanied by the escape of some substances which had previously been confined within the cell, the substances ranging from simple ions to complex molecules: for example, dissolution of the erythrocyte membrane liberates potassium ions, haemoglobin and enzymes from the cell.

When tissue death is limited and localised, and the dead tissues remain in the living individual—in other words, when necrosis occurs—some of the substances liberated from the dead cells may enter the blood-stream in detectable quantities and their determination thus becomes of clinical diagnostic importance. It has to be remembered, however, that estimations of enzyme activities are not necessarily good indications of the quantities of the enzymes actually present, and similarly, changing values of the activity of an enzyme need not always be directly related to comparable quantitative alterations of the enzyme itself, for the detected activity may have been influenced by the actions of co-enzymes and inhibitor substances.

MYOCARDIAL INFARCTION

Death of a part of the heart muscle is most commonly due to ischaemia, which, if it is sufficiently abrupt and affects a large enough area, produces an infarct from which several enzymes are liberated into the blood-stream. Of these, glutamic oxalacetic transaminase and lactic dehydrogenase activities are currently used in the laboratory as diagnostic pointers.

The activity of glutamic oxalacetic transaminase in the serum (SGOT) rises to a maximum in about twenty-four hours after infarction, thereafter falling until, after some four days, this activity is reduced to normal (Stewart *et al.*). There is an approximate relationship between the extent of the infarction and the degree of elevation of the SGOT activity.

Serum lactic dehydrogenase activity also rises rapidly with myocardial infarction, and increased activity can be detected twenty-four hours after the tissue death (Stewart *et al.*). Unlike that of SGOT, the increased activity of lactic dehydrogenase in the serum (SLD) persists for one to two weeks.

Unfortunately, neither the SGOT nor the SLD increase is associated exclusively with myocardial infarction, and similar results are apt to occur with liver disease and with injury of skeletal muscle. Elevation of SLD has also been noted when a malignant neoplasm is present: anaerobic glycolysis is a feature of malignant tumors and necrosis is not uncommonly associated with these lesions, so it is hardly surprising that lactic dehydrogenase is a prominent enzyme in the neoplastic tissues.

PULMONARY INFARCTION

A further diagnostic use for SGOT and SLD determinations has been suggested by Wacker *et al.* who have observed that in pulmonary infarction there is elevation of SLD while the SGOT remains normal, and they suggest that these findings together with an increase of serum bilirubin, are specifically indicative of infarction of lung tissue (Wacker *et al.*, 1960 and 1961).

A more detailed approach to the diagnosis of tissue necrosis, and especially myocardial necrosis, from determinations of enzymal activities in the blood, has produced some interesting advances and at the same time has revealed grounds for caution in the interpretation of the results. Taking the precautionary side first, it has been noted by Mellick that not only is an increase of SLD not a specific indication of myocardial necrosis but, since erythrocytes contain a considerably higher concentration of lactic dehydrogenase than the surrounding plasma, haemolysis, even of slight degree, will produce a falsely high result, though there will not be any additional rise in glutamic oxalacetic transaminase activity.

ENZYMAL CHANGES IN HYPOTHERMIA

That an increase of SGOT may not necessarily be associated with any evident necrosis is the conclusion of Blair and his co-workers who have studied the effects of hypothermia on the enzyme activities in the blood of dogs. The animals were anaesthetised and cooled, and the SGOT activities were determined at various stages of the experiments. Prolonged phenobarbitone anaesthesia led to only a slight rise in SGOT, and there was a similar slight rise after cooling to about 26°C. for six hours, the maximum rise occurring twenty-four hours after re-warming. Following a twelve hour period of hypothermia, however, there was a sharp rise in SGOT activity, an almost four-fold peak being found twenty-four hours after re-warming; subsequently the activity fell fairly quickly. The animals were killed and a histological search for necrosis was made in the ventricular muscle of the heart, skeletal muscle, liver, kidney and adrenal tissues, but none was found and no difference was apparent between these tissues and those from control animals.

It seems, therefore, that histologically-detectable necrosis is not essential for the production of increased SGOT activity: the prolonged cooling may perhaps modify the normal integrity of cell membranes to such an extent that, although examination by simple microscopy fails to show structural change, there may be a release of intracellular protein as well as a loss of ions from the cells.

TISSUE SPECIFICITY OF ENZYMES

Indications that greater precision may eventually be possible in the diagnosis of necrotic lesions by estimations of enzymic changes have come from Vesell *et al.*, Wroblewski *et al.*, and Dreyfus *et al.* (cited in *British Medical Journal*). The distribution of SLD activity in the globulin fractions of blood has been analysed by Vesell *et al.*, and they have found that even though the total SLD activity is unaltered in some cases, there may be a re-distribution of the activity amongst the globulin fractions in diseases associated with tissue death. Normally the maxium SLD activity is found with the α_2 fraction, but with myocardial infarction the greatest activity becomes associated with the α_1 globulin.

Five types of lactic dehydrogenase have been distinguished in the plasma by Wroblewski *et al.* (vide supra), and each of the five types of the enzyme have been found to be present in different quantities in different tissues, consequently the determination of the type of lactic dehydrogenase which is elevated in the blood can be of value as an indicator of the tissue affected by necrosis.

Another enzymic activity which is increased with myocardial necrosis is that of serum aldose, and published work on this substance also raises some hopes that this, too, may prove to be a valuable diagnostic guide. Dreyfus *et al.* (vide supra) have drawn attention to the fact that there is an aldose from muscle tissue which acts only upon fructose 1:6:diphosphate, while another aldose which is of liver origin acts on this substance and, in addition, upon fructose-1-phosphate, thus providing a potential means of distinguishing the source of an aldose in the blood.

Promising as these refined tests seem to be, there can, however, be little doubt that they will not become routine measures until reliable and relatively simple laboratory methods for their estimation are evolved.

ENZYMAL CHANGES AND THE POSTMORTEM INTERVAL

Determination of enzyme activities and of other alterations in blood taken after death have been made by Enticknap (1960) who has investigated the changes very closely and analysed the results from numerous bodies. With regard to the enzyme studies, Enticknap found that there was a postmortem rise in the activities of SGOT, serum glutamic-pyruvic transaminase (SGPT), SLD, acid and alkaline phosphatases and amylase; in general the rise was rapid at first, then it slowed and finally a fall occurred.

The initial rise in transaminase activity was established three to four hours after death and there was a fairly steady climb to high levels until about sixty hours postmortem, when diminution of activity commenced. A similar result was obtained for SLD activity, though in this case the peak of activity was not achieved until round about the fourth day. In contrast, the accumulations of the phosphatases and amylase were much less prolonged, their greatest activities occurring thirty-six to forty-eight hours postmortem.

Simultaneous investigations of the serum content of haemoglobin, phenolic substances and of the opacity of sera to ultraviolet light were also carried out. The haemoglobin rose markedly during the first twelve hours after death and continued to rise, though less quickly, until about the forty-eighth hour: the phenolic substances and the opacity rose more slowly at first but then they increased more rapidly. A transient fall of these values occurred in the forty-eight to sixty hour period, and thereafter there was a progressive accumulation with no further reduction during the periods of the investigations. The C-reactive protein levels were estimated in these cases, and no quantitative alteration was found with increasing time after death.

Not only did Enticknap find a relationship between enzymal changes and the postmortem interval, but he also established that when death was due to acute myocardial necrosis the transaminase activities fell sooner than when death was not accompanied by necrosis of heart muscle, which suggests that the release of the enzymes from the necrotic muscle into the blood-stream during the last hours of life affects the ultimate postmortem enzyme activities in the blood.

Chapter Three

POSTMORTEM NON-ENZYMAL CHEMICAL CHANGES

A VARIETY of chemical estimations have been performed by a number of investigators on specimens from cadavers, and tissues, blood and cerebro-spinal fluid have been examined. The main objects have been to discover whether any of the tests are of use in determining the time of death, the cause of death, or the biochemical state prior to death.

THE TIME OF DEATH

The potassium and urea levels of postmortem blood were measured by Kevorkian *et al.* in an investigation into the use of cadaver blood for transfusion purposes: the concentrations of both substances were found to be raised. In one case the potassium was 13 mEq per litre in blood taken four and one-half hours postmortem, in another case where blood was taken six hours after death the potassium had risen to 13.6 mEq per litre, while in a third case it reached 24 mEq per litre, five and one-half hours after death. These levels, which are clearly raised and evidently rising, compare with the 30 mEq reported in stored blood from living donors. The results obtained by these workers for the urea will be given later (vide infra).

The most immediate source of the potassium found in postmortem blood is the mass of erythrocytes, from which potassium is liberated as haemolysis proceeds, and in the early part of the postmortem period the serum potassium is thus an indirect indicator of the degree of haemolysis which had taken place by the time the sample was obtained. The erythrocytes are not, however, the only source of potassium for after death there is a general release of the substance from cells. For example, cerebro-spinal fluid is hardly likely to be affected by haemolysis fairly soon after death, provided that no intra-cranial haemorrhage is present, for the fluid is not in immediate continuity with blood: Mason *et al.* examined postmortem cerebro-spinal fluids for potassium to see whether the results might therefore give some indication of the antemortem cerebro-spinal fluid levels of this element. The finding showed, in the event, that there was a sharp rise of potassium in the fluid during the postmortem period under investigation (up to 70 hours) which could be expressed in a linear fashion, but there were considerable variations in the levels of the potassium from different bodies at corresponding postmortem intervals.

The concentration of phosphate has been measured in the cerebro-spinal fluid and in the blood serum by Schleyer *et al.* In each case a rise was found after death, but although the initial increases were found to be regular, the rises soon became too irregular for them to be used for calculating the time of death.

An attempt has been made by Schourup (cited by Mant, 1953) to find a relationship between a combination of several of the postmortem chemical changes found in the cerebro-spinal fluid of adults and the time of death: amino-acids, lactic acid and non-protein nitrogen values were included with the axillary temperature in an arithmetical formula. Provided that the postmortem interval did not exceed fifteen hours, a high degree of success was claimed for the method.

The investigation by Kevorkian and co-workers on the potassium and urea levels in cadaver blood, to which reference has been made above, showed that the urea rose as the time after death increased. At two and one-half hours postmortem the urea was 11.2mg. per 100ml. of blood: the level was 14.7mg. in blood from a second body taken after five and one-half hours, while in the third case 6-hour blood contained 34.3mg. per 100ml.

URAEMIA

Uraemia is a cause of death which may produce little in the way of specific autopsy findings other than a characteristic odour which is not always readily appreciable. Personal investigations of the postmortem blood urea in such cases have been made, with blood from non-uraemic bodies as controls. The blood urea was found to be elevated in the uraemic bodies to a greater extent than in the controls.

A more extensive study of the postmortem chemical changes in uraemia has more recently been made by Jenkins, who determined the urea in blood and in the cerebro-spinal fluid in uraemic and in control cases. He found that the blood urea rose after death, but in a manner which was irregular and unrelated both to the time after death at which the sample was taken and, when it was known, to the blood urea in the agonal period. It was suggested that some of the increase in blood urea might be due to the continued formation of urea by the liver after somatic death, while falsely high and rising values could be due to ammonia (which is produced after death) reacting in the urease-nesslerization technique employed for the determination of urea. The cerebro-spinal fluid urea was found to rise several hours after an elevation of the blood urea was noted, and the point was made that the lag in the rise of cerebro-spinal fluid urea was particularly marked when a moribund state was accompanied by a failing circulation of blood through the choroidal plexuses. Jenkins found a good correlation between the postmortem cerebro-spinal fluid and blood urea and the ante-mortem blood urea in cases of uraemia, the postmortem urea levels being markedly elevated.

Schott estimated urea and non-protein nitrogen in the

myocardium and found these substances to be increased in uraemic cases.

An altogether different approach to the chemical diagnosis of uraemia in the cadaver has been made by Csaszar *et al.*, who reported that indican could be found in the cerebro-spinal fluid from uraemic bodies, the test giving a negative result when uraemia was absent, or, it is claimed, if uraemia of extra-renal cause had been present.

ANOXIA

A good deal of attention has been given recently to the detection of lactic acid in postmortem tissues, in order to decide whether this might be a guide to the existence of anoxia or hypoxia immediately before death. The anaerobic metabolism of glucose produces lactic acid, and the latter can be detected reasonably easily in brain tissue obtained after death.

Estimations of the lactic acid content of tissue samples from the brains of dogs, rabbits and rats which had been subjected to terminal hypoxia showed that the lactic acid was raised above normal, and the degree to which the lactic acid was elevated was found to be related to the species of animal as well as to the intensity and duration of the oxygen deprivation: the raised level of lactic acid persisted after death for the duration of the experiments. Animals which had been rendered hypoxic and then restored to normal oxygen conditions so that they recovered from the hypoxic phase, were found to have normal postmortem levels of brain lactic acid (van Fossan *et al.*).

Biddulph and others, working with dogs, showed that the lactic acid concentration was higher in the gray than in the white matter of the brain: they also demonstrated that hypo-capnia alone did not result in significant alterations in the lactic acid content, but hypoxia with or without hypocapnia regularly raised the brain lactic acid.

HYPERGLYCAEMIA

The investigations were pursued and extended by Dominguez and co-workers, who confirmed the association between the postmortem cerebral lactic acid concentration and agonal hypoxia. These researchers also examined the effects of antemortem variations of blood glucose upon postmortem brain lactic acid. A rise in blood glucose results in an increase of glucose in the brain, and this will cause an additional amount of lactic acid to be formed by postmortem breakdown of the sugar. An increase in the lactic acid content of the brain has therefore to be regarded as no more than an indication of agonal hyperglycaemia.

It is noteworthy that asphyxia causes hyperglycaemia, but other acute conditions, in particular trauma, are also accompanied by raised blood glucose, and if death should occur under these conditions, the brain lactic acid will be elevated. Rats which were rendered hypoglycaemic and then anoxic had no increase in the lactic acid content of their brains.

It seems clear, then, that while the level of brain lactic acid will reveal agonal hyperglycaemia, it is not a specific indication of hypoxia.

The direct determination of glucose in postmortem blood is possible, but the examination is of value in relation to the agonal level of blood glucose only if it is made immediately after somatic death, or certainly within two hours of death (Hill).

When glycogen was present in the liver in any quantity at the time of death, the substance will persist in this organ after death where its presence can be demonstrated chemically and histologically, though after some hours of postmortem change histochemistry may seem to reveal more of the glycogen than that detected by simple chemical analysis (Morrione *et al.*). The hepatic glycogen falls off rapidly at first, regardless of the initial concentration of the substance, but thereafter the decrement is fairly slow. During the early hours of hepatic glycogen loss in the intact dead body, the blood glucose is found to be higher in samples taken from the right side of the heart than in those from the left, the sugar having diffused thence from the liver. Glucose is also formed after death from muscle glycogen.

SERUM OPACITY

During the agonal period there is an increasing opacity of the serum to ultraviolet light, a phenomenon which persists after the serum proteins have been precipitated. After death a similar opacity occurs (Enticknap, 1960), which has been related to the accumulation of serum organic acids. Laves found that the ultraviolet absorption curves of postmortem sera differed from those of blood taken during life, as the maximum absorption passed towards the shorter wavelengths commencing at 250mμ rather than the longer at 285mμ. The absorption increased as the shift from longer to shorter wavelength took place. Haemolysis was excluded as a causative factor in this phenomenon.

CORONARY OCCLUSION

Turbidity of postmortem serum is related to a particular cause of death—coronary occlusion (Enticknap, 1961), the blood lipids of the bodies of those dying from this cause being significantly raised.

There is a natural increase in serum lipids after death, the rate of which is given by Enticknap as rather less than ½ per cent per hour, but the elevations found in the cases of coronary occlusion were well above the expected normal postmortem values associated with other causes of death. When necrosis of the myocardium was present at the time of death there was much less elevation of the lipid levels. During the course of this investigation, it was noticed that there was no consistent relationship between the blood lipids (cholesterol, fatty acids and lipoprotein) and the quantity or nature of the stomach contents. There is, quite clearly, a postmortem biochemical pattern related to coronary occlusive deaths.

The postmortem levels of cholesterol in serum have also been investigated by Glanville, who compared the antemortem and postmortem values of serum cholesterol in twenty-six subjects. A sufficiently good correspondence was found between the results for the postmortem levels to be taken as reliable indicators of the antemortem values.

While admitting that, despite the various attempts made so far, a precise and reliable chemical (or biological) clock which will show the time of death, regardless of the magnitude of the interval, has yet to be discovered, there is, however, no reason to suggest that postmortem chemistry is, and will continue to be, only of scant value. This type of investigation offers the possibility of accurate deductions of some antemortem states, and it may, in certain conditions, even assist in assessing the cause of death. As chemical analyses of cadaver specimens increase in frequency and range, so will the establishment of normal postmortem chemical values allow increasing accuracy to attend inferences made of antemortem conditions.

Chapter Four

RIGOR MORTIS

AN EARLY and obvious postmortem change is rigor mortis, a state in which there is stiffening of the muscles, both involuntary and voluntary, and regardless of their size. Under normal circumstances rigor commences about two hours after death and it persists for some thirty hours or so before the muscles soften and the stiffness passes off.

THE ADENOSINE TRIPHOSPHATE CYCLE

At one time it was believed that the lactic acid which accumulates in muscle after death was in some way responsible for the rigor, but recent work on the chemistry of the contraction and relaxation of living muscle has opened wider fields in the study of the processes in dead muscle. The key to the problem of rigor mortis now appears to be the adenosine triphosphate cycle.

The dephosphorylation of adenosine triphosphate (ATP) by the action of ATPase produces adenosine diphosphate (ADP) and phosphate, together with a large amount of energy which is available for cellular activities during life: in muscle cells, energy from this source is utilized for the production of contraction. The recurring loss of ATP is made good during life by resynthesis, ADP, phosphocreatine (PC) and glycogen contributing to the reaction; by this process energy is transferred from glycogen to PC and thence to ATP.

Resting muscle cells remain relaxed and elastic as long

as there is a sufficiency of ATP. Reduction of the ATP to a critical level brings about contraction, but the relaxed state will be regained if the appropriate quantities of PC and glycogen are available for the restoration of phosphate to the ADP.

POSTMORTEM LOSS OF ATP

There is usually enough ATP in muscle at the time of somatic death to maintain relaxation, but after death the ATP is progressively and irreversibly destroyed. There is no resynthesis of ATP in dead muscle, and the loss of ATP by postmortem change cannot therefore be made good spontaneously. The postmortem alteration of ATP has been shown to be due to a combination of dephosphorylation and deamination (Callow), so that in dead muscle the chief product from ATP breakdown is inosine monophosphate (IMP) rather than ADP, and traces of inosine di- and triphosphate are also formed.

When these destructive postmortem changes reduce the ATP to a critical level the muscle can no longer remain relaxed, consequently it contracts: in other words, rigor mortis has commenced.

Rigor persists naturally until decomposition of the proteins of the muscle fibres renders them incapable of any further contractive effort, and the muscles then soften and so appear to relax. The irreversibility of the postmortem breakdown of ATP means that rigor can occur only once in a muscle in natural circumstances.

Rigor may be abolished experimentally and the muscle induced to relax again if the ATP deficit is made good by the addition of ATP together with magnesium (for the active form is an Mg-ATP complex) and an inhibitor substance to prevent the too-rapid loss of the added ATP. The amount of ATP needed to reverse rigor by this means is approximately the same as that known to exist in intact muscle when rigor begins (Callow).

FACTORS INFLUENCING THE TIMING OF RIGOR MORTIS

The time of onset of rigor mortis depends to a large extent upon the amount of ATP in the muscle at the moment of somatic death. Strenuous muscular activity shortly before death, especially if it brings about an oxygen "debt," will lead to diminution of the muscle ATP and glycogen, and the immediate resynthesis of ATP will be reduced. In such circumstances the muscle ATP is already somewhat depleted at the time of death, therefore the postmortem critical level of ATP will be reached more rapidly than normal and rigor will appear earlier.

Increase in the temperature of the body hastens the breakdown of ATP and, in life, it accelerates the metabolism of glycogen, so that a terminal pyrexia will tend to bring the onset of rigor nearer to the time of death.

Generalised rigor may rarely occur virtually at the time of death if intense metabolic demands had been operating just before death: such "instantaneous" rigor can result in the body maintaining its agonal posture. In occasional cases a few muscles may pass into rigor at the time of death, well before generalised rigor commences, constituting the so-called "cadaveric spasm." This local rigor which so rapidly affects groups of associated muscles may well be based upon the relative exhaustion of ATP and glycogen in those muscles, due to unduly severe and prolonged contraction immediately prior to death.

The onset of rigor is delayed by freezing the muscles, and, providing that the muscle cells are not damaged by the freezing process, rigor can appear after thawing.

Gallo has shown that there is a decrease in PC in the heart muscle of animals when anoxic conditions are operating: thus it seems that oxygen lack alone may play some part in determining the time of the onset of rigor. Investigations of the occurrence of rigor mortis in the myocardium of the rabbit and the ox showed also that the rigidity does not occur uniformly throughout the muscle: instead, the rigor commences in a number of foci which increase until decomposition halts the process (Gallo). The concentrations of ATP and PC were found to be lower in these foci than elsewhere in the myocardium, due, to some extent at least, to the slower oxygenation in these regions because of their distance from a plentiful capillary blood supply. How far these observations may apply to skeletal and other muscle remains to be seen.

Chapter Five

CHEMISTRY AND DATING

A SPECIALISED application of postmortem analytical chemical and radiochemical methods is to the investigation of long-dead remains in order to ascertain their antiquity. While this is in a way an assessment of the time of death, the circumstances and details of the investigation differ so greatly from those which normally apply to recently-dead bodies that this particular field of postmortem chemical change is best considered as a separate topic.

INTRINSIC ORGANIC SUBSTANCES

In the dating of ancient remains, attention has to be concentrated upon the hard tissues. After the destructive changes of decomposition in buried tissues have run their course, the surviving hard tissues offer little in the way of morphological findings from which the time of death or burial may be assessed with any accuracy, and in these circumstances chemical investigations assume great importance. The loss of organic constituents from the relatively protected cavities within bones and teeth buried in soil depends upon the degree to which postmortem decomposition has progressed, which in turn is a function of time, and upon the nature and conditions of the soil in which the specimens have been buried. Ordinarily the organic nitrogenous substances of the body, such as collagen, are markedly diminished in oxidising conditions and organic carbon

34

and fat are also lost, while reducing conditions are less destructive to these tissue constituents.

It could be expected that postmortem changes would ultimately bring about the complete alteration of the organic part of bone, but analyses of fossilised human and mammoth bones have shown that there is a surprising survival of organic nitrogenous compounds in these bones, and it is easily demonstrated that in recent-to-fairly-old bones there is a sufficient organic content to give rise to the characteristic smell when the bones are heated by sawing or by drilling.

An investigation of the nature of the organic compounds present in fairly-old-to-very-old bones (roughly 1,510 to 5,385 years old) disclosed amino acids in all but two specimens. Two-dimensional paper chromatography detected aspartic acid, glycine and glutamic acid in some specimens, together with various other amino acids, while only aspartic acid was found in one very old specimen (Ezra *et al.*, 1957). The isolation of gelatin from deer antlers, estimated to be 12,000 years old, has also been reported (Sinex *et al.*). Analysis of compact bone from a frozen Alaskan mammoth, dead for several thousand years, showed that the total nitrogen and the acid-extractable carbonate were quantitatively what would be expected in fresh bone (Ezra *et al.*, 1959). Evidently some of the constituents of protein can survive in bone for very long periods of time under the differing circumstances of fossilisation and freezing. It is too soon, however, to be able to apply the results of these estimations to the accurate dating of bone, as the rates at which the loss of amino acids occur have yet to be established.

ABSORBED EXTRINSIC SUBSTANCES

The chemical results most utilised so far in dating remains depend upon the detection of substances which have incidentally become part of the tissues and are in no way products of postmortem changes of the tissues.

A number of compounds which happen to be present in

soil gradually seep into buried remains and they may become incorporated in the tissues; this process is often very slow and its rate is apt to be unreliably variable, so that while the quantitative determination of any chemical contaminants acquired in this manner is of some use in dating buried remains, the results are so uncertain that they are better applied to the estimation of relative rather than of absolute time intervals. A particular use for this method of dating remains lies in the assessment of the contemporaniety of a number of remains found buried together in a single locus.

Estimations of time intervals calculated from the concentrations of soil constituents in tissues refer only to the period during which the tissues remained buried (assuming that the absorption has been possible during the whole of this time), and not to the lapse of time since death, for these two periods may differ significantly. The significance of datings obtained from determinations of postmortem chemical contaminants in tissues differs, therefore, very greatly from those calculated from the tissue content of radioactive carbon, for the latter is related to the time interval actually from death (see page 38).

Apart from substances which occur naturally in soils, buried remains may absorb chemicals which have been applied to the soil, such as artificial and natural fertilisers, weed-killers and the like, and in certain circumstances the detection of contamination of this nature could be critical.

Some compounds diffuse much more quickly than others from soil into remains (arsenicals are noteworthy examples of this), the contaminants soon reaching appreciable levels in the superficial tissues of a body. It might well be that a systematic study of the nature of rapidly-absorbed compounds and the rates at which they are taken up by tissues in different circumstances could provide some guide to the duration of relatively brief burials.

The use of various chemical analyses of ancient bones and

teeth in dating has been mentioned in an account of the investigations of the remains found at Piltdown, the attention naturally being upon the changes which are found in fossilised remains. Attention is drawn to the accumulation of fluorine and uranium in specimens (the substances being derived from extraneous sources), as well as to the intrinsic alterations in the nitrogen, carbon and fat of bones and teeth after various postmortem intervals (Weiner *et al.*).

Fluorine compounds in the soil are absorbed by bones and teeth which have remained buried for long periods of time. The relationship between the duration of burial and the concentration of fluorine in the tissues was investigated by Middleton in 1844 and then by Carnot in 1893. It is quite clear from these early researches as well as from those published more recently (e.g., Oakley 1949; Oakley *et al.* (in Weiner *et al.*)), that there is too great a variation in the concentration of soil fluorine and in its rate of uptake by tissues for assessments of datings derived from fluorine estimations to be expressed in absolute terms with any confidence. A further difficulty, and one to which scant attention seems to have been given, is that the variations of the chemical nature of bone due to postmortem ageing are not yet known with precision, consequently the determination of the fluorine content may be more subject to error than is usually accepted.

The absorption of uranium by buried hard tissues is, like that of fluorine, slow and variable. The tissues absorb and retain uranium from soil and water, and as the concentration of the substance builds up in the tissues so the radioactivity of the tissues increases. At the same time new radioactive elements are continuously being produced at a steady rate by the disintegrating uranium and it might seem that a mathematical relationship could be determined between the total radioactivity and the postmortem age of bone or tooth, but this hope is doomed because of the uncertainties and irregularities attendant upon the initial and subsequently con-

tinued uptake of uranium from the soil. Measurement of the
tissue radioactivity derived from absorbed uranium can provide no more than a means of estimating relative time intervals.

Precise dating from the investigations mentioned briefly
above cannot be achieved, and even when the time intervals
applicable to several specimens in a purely relative manner
are to be determined it is necessary to employ as many of
the chemical and radiochemical estimations as the sizes
of the specimens permit in order to reduce uncertainty to
a minimum.

CARBON-14

Greater precision in absolute terms can be reached by
the methods which relate the radioactivity of tissues due to
their radioactive carbon to the time which the tissues have
been dead.

Amongst the effects of cosmic rays on the atmosphere is
the production of radioactive carbon (carbon-14; C-14), and
at the present time a steady state has been reached in which
the rate at which the C-14 decays is balanced by the rate at
which the element is formed. Living organic matter is in-
volved in a metabolic carbon cycle, and a quantity of C-14
accumulates in the living organism from the natural assimi-
lation of carbon compounds which come from organic
sources and therefore contain a proportion of the radioactive
element. The C-14 content of the organism is steadily
maintained for as long as it lives, but as soon as death occurs
the cycle is broken for that particular organism because its
metabolism ceases, and since C-14 is continually, though
slowly, disintegrating the amount of C-14 in the dead tissues
becomes gradually less and less.

The postmortem loss of C-14 has been studied by Libby,
who developed a method for assessing the length of time
that an organism had been dead from measurements of its
C-14 content. The half-life of C-14 is in the order of 5,600

years, thus at the end of this period any radioactivity due to C-14 will have become halved, because during that time half the initial quantity of the C-14 will have disintegrated. The unit amount of radioactivity from C-14 at the time of death of organisms is known, hence the measurement of the C-14 content of the tissues after death is a guide to the time of death within certain limits.

A simple carbon compound, such as carbon dioxide or acetylene, or even carbon itself, is prepared from the tissues to be dated, and the radioactivity is then estimated. It is, of course, necessary to avoid contamination of the specimen during its collection, and essential to ensure that the carbon being used for the test is derived solely from the tissues under investigation.

The contamination of the atmosphere with radioactive substances from atomic explosions may ultimately affect the accuracy of dating based upon C-14 determinations, yet it may also offer a new line of approach since some radioactive substances, such as strontium, are held in an active form in tissues during life and after death, and the finding of these substances in postmortem tissues would indicate that death had occurred after atmospheric contamination had been produced, provided that postmortem contamination from other sources, such as the soil, could be excluded.

Chapter Six

THE SPONTANEOUS INHIBITION OF
POSTMORTEM CHANGES: ADIPOCERE

T his form of postmortem change is that in which there is alteration of the appearance and consistency of the fatty tissues of the body consequent upon the transformation of the neutral fat into new compounds, mostly fatty acids.

This change, although it must have been observed very many years ago, received scant attention until comparatively recent times. The word "adipocere" was introduced into the literature of the subject in 1786, but before this time it was believed that there was some association between postmortem changes and the production of fatty materials, and it had been observed too, that the spontaneous preservation of bodies would sometimes occur without the obvious changes of mummification.

THE HISTORY OF SPONTANEOUS PRESERVATION

An instance of the persistence of a body in a recognisable form for a very long period of time is given in the account of the relics of St. Cuthbert, edited by Battiscombe. Cuthbert died in 687 A.D. after an exhausting illness which lasted for three weeks: his body was washed after death, clad in robes and headcloth, and placed in a stone sarcophagus on Lindisfarne. The tomb was opened eleven years later, when the body, which was found to be "incorrupt," was re-vested and the headcloth removed. The body was then left in peace until 875, when it was again removed from the tomb and then transported around Northern England for a period which is now unknown. The coffin in which the body then lay may have been opened in about 944, during the time of King Edmund, and it was possibly opened again some twenty or thirty years later. There is no record of the condition of the body at this time, but it is known that at one stage the bones of the venerable Bede were placed in the coffin by Aelfred, and it seems reasonably certain that when the body of the Saint was seen yet again in 1104 it was then by no means just a skeleton. In fact Cuthbert's body was said to have been intact in 1537-8, when it was seen during the time of the sacerdotal upheavals in the time of Henry VIII, a period when considerable damage could have been wrought upon the coffin and the remains within: however there does not seem to be any mention of deliberate spoiling of the body, which by then had remained in an apparently good state for something like 850 years. Further exhumations were performed and by 1827 the body had become a skeleton, a finding which was confirmed in 1899.

If the old accounts are to be believed, the body of St. Cuthbert persisted in an un-decomposed state for very many years without artificial preservation. Were this so, then the likeliest explanation would be that adipocere had formed with consequent spontaneous preservation of the greater part of the body tissues, but this can only be inferred for there is no accurate description of the body until it had become merely a skeleton.

An interesting point which may also be raised, and one which is brought forward in the account of the Relics, is that an odour of "sweetest fragrancy" was perceived when the coffin was opened at various times. This may have been an expression of piety on the part of the observers, whose standards of fragrance may not have been as exquisite as those of modern times, or it might have been some indication that aromatic substances had been employed in the preparation of the body, for an echo of the Egyptian methods of embalming was to be found in the preparations for some early Christian burials. Support for the suggestion that a form of embalming had been used on Cuthbert's body is found in the fact that bandages had been tightly applied to the head and neck.

An old account by Collignon of the exhumation of a body, possibly that of Thomas Beaufort uncle of King Henry V, describes the remains as being well preserved with the muscles in a good state, the brain recognisable and some lung tissue probably present. The abdominal cavity was found to be empty of viscera, from which it was concluded that partial evisceration had been performed. The body had been buried in a leaden coffin in the soil beneath the choir of the abbey at St. Edmund's-Bury in Suffolk for between 200 and 300 years, and although there is, unfortunately, no mention of the body fat, it is quite likely that adipocere had been present.

Collignon, who was Professor of Anatomy at Cambridge, was uncertain as to whether any artificial means of preservation had been applied to the body, but he expressed some scepticism of the value of embalming, believing that natural causes alone might account for the preservation of bodies which had long lain dead. He remarked upon the accounts of bodies which had been found little changed after prolonged interment, apparently without artificial means of preservation, and it had occurred to him that factors might be discovered which could influence the spontaneous preservation of bodies. To this end Collignon suggested that the age, sex and terminal illness of the deceased, the nature of the soil and the situation of the burial might, on investigation, be related to the natural fate of a body after death. Had the Professor pursued this theory it is quite possible that he would have advanced the understanding of post-mortem changes very considerably.

Bacon in his collection of curiously diverse comments on natural history made occasional remarks on postmortem changes, though not always with the clarity one might desire, and he has recorded that almost all "flesh" may be turned into fat after death. This conclusion seems to have been derived from the observation of the extraction of fat from meat by the heat from boiling water, an experiment which Bacon (VI) describes as something of a novelty, though as a fact it was probably well known beforehand to generations of housewives whose duties precluded much literacy.

Bacon believed that there was a direct alteration of muscle into fat, and it is interesting that it was thought that the fatty substances of adipocere also formed from muscle until it was eventually shown that adipocere is formed by a chemical change of fatty tissue, a revelation which did not come until the beginning of the nineteenth century. There does not seem to be any reason to suppose that Bacon was aware of postmortem changes in fat. This oversight, however, does not greatly diminish the historical value of Bacon's records of his investigations into postmortem changes, for he established that the changes were inhibited by cold (Bacon II) and by dehydration (Bacon III), while they were accelerated by churchyard earth (Bacon IV). He made no notes on the action of sunlight upon dead tissues (see page 6), but he did suggest an experiment whereby the effect of moonbeams upon putrefaction might be investigated (Bacon V).

An experimental rather than a speculative approach to the problem of non-putrefied, non-mummified bodies was begun by Fourcroy in 1785 and the succeeding years. This investigator was aware that postmortem changes could be accompanied by an apparent increase in the fat content of some tissues, and had recorded, for example, that a piece of liver had become fatty, smooth and unctuous after suspension in the air in the laboratory for ten years: Fourcroy had also found that potassium lye "dissolved" part of this liver, forming a soap. There is no mention of any degree of ante-mortem fatty change, which could well have been present in that liver before the experiment was begun.

A distinction was made by Fourcroy between the fatty substances of gall-stones, which he called "spermacetti," and that of cadavers, which he called "adipocere" because of the fatty and waxy nature of the substance.

Fourcroy collected examples of adipocere from bodies exhumed from graves and "ditch" burials in a cemetery fifteen years after the interments. The adipocere was found to have a melting point of 52.5°C. and to consist of ammonia soap with calcium phosphate and fat: it was thought that the substance was a product of the putrefaction of all the non-keratinous and non-bony tissues.

A summary of the discoveries and experiments on the nature of adipocere, commencing with those of Fourcroy, was brought out in 1860 by Wetherill who showed how scientific interest in this substance awakened during those seventy-five years.

In 1794, Gibbes immersed tissues in running water in an attempt to produce adipocere, and he was of the opinion that the change could also be brought about in a few days by the action of nitric acid on tissues. There was, however, confusion over the distinction between neutral fat and adipocere, and from the results obtained when Bostock repeated the experiments in 1803 it seems clear that the substance which was supposed to have been manufactured from the tissues was much more like neutral fat than adipocere.

Up to this time the origin of adipocere was a mystery and it was generally thought to be derived in some way from all the soft tissues, but correction came nine years later when Chevreul showed that "churchyard fat" contained fatty acids, a yellow pigment and odourous substances together with lime, potassium salts, iron oxide, lactates and nitrogenous substances. Chevreul concluded that the fatty acids were derived solely from neutral fat in the adipose tissues by the action of ammonia, the latter compound subsequently vanishing.

Assent to this solution of the problem was given by Gay Lussac, who further showed that finely-chopped muscle from which fat had been extracted by ether did not form adipocere in water.

This conclusion was a sad blow to those who were convinced that adipocere was a product of decomposed muscle and other non-fatty tissues, for amongst their aspirations was the proposition that the controlled hydrolysis of muscle unsuitable for human consumption would be a valuable means of preparing commercial fats. Even had the process worked, this hope was doomed because Harkol found that the "foetid mass" from bodies buried in moist soil was incapable of being made into candles, the principal use anticipated for the adipocere.

Wetherill himself put forward some observations on the presence of adipocere in the bodies of adults exhumed from low-lying wet soil in an American graveyard; the affected bodies were well nourished, and no adipocere was seen in the remains of children.

At the turn of the nineteenth century an account appeared concerning the recovery of the body of a young woman from an English river in which the remains had been immersed for just on a year (Mansfield). This was a paper which Wetherill had neglected to include in his survey. No soft tissues remained about the head, neck or thorax, but the abdominal wall was preserved, as were also the abdominal viscera, the thighs and the legs. There appeared to be a thick covering of fat on the preserved regions, this fatty layer being "cracked" in such a way as to resemble the peel of a walnut. The substance of the layer was white and it seemed to merge with the deeper muscles: where the white covering was deficient, the deeper tissues were described as having the appearance and substance of boiled ham. The soft tissues were said to have had a most offensive odour.

This may well be the earliest English account of an adipocerous body in which attention is drawn specifically to the distribution and condition of the fat: there is, however, no speculation about the phenomenon, no suggestion of a special name for the fatty substance and no reference to the findings and experiments of others.

During the year before the appearance of Wetherill's review, another American author, Dalton, published a description of adipocere in one of several bodies so affected. The burials had taken place about twenty-seven years previously. The site had been a cholera pit into which the coffined remains had been stacked, commencing at a depth of twenty feet, and the uppermost of the thirteen or fourteen tiers of coffins were covered by some three or four feet of soil. Adipocere was found in those bodies buried at the level of the water mark.

The adipocere had a cheesy consistency with a fairly strong odour in which earthy, cheesy and ammoniacal constituents blended, the smell of ammonia being the most persistent.

It was suggested that ammonia was produced by decomposing muscle and became available for the production of ammoniacal soap from the fat, and the observation that adipocere is commoner in bodies buried in a communal grave than in isolated burials was explained by assuming that in the latter case ammonia in solution diffused away into the soil and was lost from the body; when many bodies lay together this diffusion would serve more to distribute the ammonia solution amongst the bodies. Dalton did not believe that adipocere formed in bodies which were totally and continuously immersed in water.

A number of reports of the finding of adipocere in bodies from burials and from water followed (e.g., Tripp; Manson; Gandy; Mitchell) but little or nothing was added to the prevailing knowledge of the topic until 1927, when Barral saw adipocere in two bodies only fifteen days and three months respectively after death, thus introducing the fact that this change could occur far more quickly than had hitherto been accepted.

In this same year came an histochemical study of adipocere formation by Kernbach and his co-workers, who paid particular attention to the changes seen in body fat at intervals after death. Histological sections were cut from frozen blocks of the fat, some of the blocks being quite unfixed, while some were fixed in formalin and yet others in Ciaccio's fluid.

These workers noted changes in the fatty tissues in bodies which had been immersed in water for seven to ten days: small droplets of fat filled the adipose cells, rather than the large, uniformly-staining intracellular masses of fat seen shortly after the death of fat cells. Staining with Nile blue sulphate no longer produced the rosy metachromasia of fresh fat, red islets and violet and blue tints now being seen. The formation of the tiny droplets of fat was called "fragmentation," and this, and the variable results with Nile blue sulphate, became more intense in bodies dead for longer periods of time.

The progressive loss of the ability of the fat to produce the normal reactions with standard stains for fat, and the loss of metachromasia on Nile blue staining indicated the disappearance of neutral fat, and it was assumed that fatty acids (probably of the unsaturated varieties) and soaps were forming. By about the fifteenth day after death, all metachromasia with Nile blue was lost and the tissues stained a deep blue with this dye. Reactions for fatty acids were now obtained with copper acetate and with Fischler's reagent, and crystals were seen in the tissues. These crystals were thought to be soaps, and it was recorded that the soaps vanished after the eightieth day postmortem, although the fatty acids still remained when all the soaps had gone.

Further discussions on the composition of adipocere were published (e.g., Biancalani *et al.*) and crystals in the tissues were again described by Klauer *et al.* in 1937.

ADIPOCERE FORMATION IN DRY AND
RELATIVELY DRY ENVIRONMENTS

In 1946, an account was produced by Macleod of the condition of 335 male bodies of war-time victims who had been shot. These bodies were clothed and they had been stacked in piles in caves: the exhumations were carried out four months later. It was found that the bodies from the tops of the piles had little or no adipocere and most were putrefied while some were possibly mummified, but adipocerous changes were much in evidence in the other bodies. The adipocere was found mainly in the skin of the anterior wall of the abdomen and of the lower limbs; no complete example of the formation of adipocere in all the sites of body fat was seen, and no adipocere was found in any internal organs. The greatest amounts of adipocere were present in the larger bodies, and the older victims were less decomposed than the younger. Clothing was found to have delayed putrefactive changes.

Macleod formed the view that the conditions which most favoured adipocere formation were adiposity, moisture, still air, lack of oxygen and cessation of bacterial growth. The offensive and powerful smell of the remains was emphasised.

Four years later, in 1950, another account appeared of the postmortem changes found in the bodies of more war victims (Mant, 1950). These bodies were exhumed from a variety of graves and the important findings relating to adipocere were that this change was a not uncommon finding, that it could occur in bodies buried in graves that were neither waterlogged nor particularly wet, and it was a change that could be found in bodies buried for as short a time as one year, as well as in bodies from burials of longer duration.

There was some relationship between postmortem change and the state of the body at the time of death, well-nourished bodies being better preserved than those sparely covered. Bodies buried in large coffins containing a thick layer of wood shavings decomposed more rapidly than those buried for the same length of time without coffins. Adipocere was found far more often in the non-coffined burials. Where bodies, or parts of bodies, were covered by clothing, adipocere was more frequent, and the same finding was noted in mass graves where bodies had lain in contact with each other.

It seemed reasonable to infer that adipocere formed not only when there was abundant extraneous water, but also when there was relatively little additional moisture. If this were true, then it could be supposed that at least some of the tissue fluid had been utilised in the hydrolysis of fat to adipocere, and strong support for this theory was afforded by the fact that the non-fatty tissues were dry and to some extent "mummified."

That decomposition accompanied burial in deep, roomy coffins with a good deal of wood shavings was explained by the rise of temperature due to the fermentation of the wood as it became damp.

It was clear that exposure to air after burial also affected the nature of postmortem changes, for bodies with an initially good or reasonable degree of spontaneous preservation decomposed quickly once air was admitted to the grave. There was no particular correlation between the type of soil in which bodies were buried and the frequency of the formation of adipocere.

Mant later recorded some further instances of adipocere formation which strengthened the theory that an abundance of extracorporeal water was not essential for much hydrolysis of body fat to occur, and he cited one case in which adipocere was found to be widespread in the body of a man suspended from a tree by a rope (Mant, 1957).

Very useful opportunities for the personal study of exhumations were offered when two sets of vaults were opened in order that the bodies inhumed there might be re-interred elsewhere in new coffins (Evans, 1963). The vaults were in different geographical situations; they were well constructed of brick and were dry, and a steady state had maintained in the vaults from the time of the burials until the exhumations. In neither set of vaults were the coffins interred in the earth.

THE FREQUENCY OF ADIPOCERE IN
DRY ENVIRONMENTS

Detailed analyses of results could not be given for the first set of exhumations because circumstances precluded exhaustive study of the many factors relating to the remains, for example the records of the deaths and burials were not available, but even so it was quite evident that more than half the number of the inhumed bodies had extensive adipocere. These remains had been in the vaults between 100 and 150 years, and there was no suggestion that the conditions in the vaults had been anything but dry for the whole of this period.

Fortunately it was possible to make fairly extensive investigations relating to the inhumations in the second set of vaults, for the sex, age and date of death were known for all the remains observed, and for all but four the date of inhumation was given so that the time during which nearly all the bodies had lain dead before inhumation could be calculated: the prevailing climatic conditions during those "pre-inhumation" periods were made available by the Meteorological Office. For some of the bodies there were records of the supposed cause of death, but these were found to be too vague to be of any use.

In this series, thirty-three of the remains showed much adipocere, and this was associated with good spontaneous preservation: the other remains, twenty-six in number, had decomposed to skeletons. No indication of artificial preservation was seen in any of these bodies and there was no reason to suppose that any of the changes were not spontaneous.

Thus adipocere had formed in 56 per cent of the fifty-nine remains examined, and it is now quite certain that this change is not a rarity in these conditions.

There was no doubt that the vaults had been dry during the 103 to 127 years of inhumation, and as the coffins were well made and none contained any excess of sawdust it seemed evident that virtually all the water required for the production of adipocere had been derived from the body tissues. In fact the non-fatty body tissues were found to be in a dehydrated state.

THE PERVIOUSNESS OF COFFINS

An interesting incidental finding arose concerning the soundness of the coffins. The coffins consisted in all but two instances of an inner and an outer stout wooden box separated by a sealed lead shell, and most of the inner boxes and lead shells appeared to be intact although a number of the outer boxes had broken: the impression was that the remains lay in completely enveloping, almost certainly impervious enclosures, but this idea was shattered by the discovery of living larvae of Tinea pallescentella (the Greater Pale clothes moth) in one coffin. It was discovered that these exploratory larvae had entered the triple coffin quite recently by way of cracks and apertures in the wooden and leaden coverings, their portals of entry being demonstrated when the coffin was filled with water, which ran freely through the minute holes. The larvae had been attracted to the keratin of the scalp hair of the body, on which they subsequently flourished and developed to perfect insects in the laboratory. Obviously even a triple coffin stored in a sheltered, dry and cool environment eventually becomes permeable.

FACTORS IN ADIPOCERE FORMATION

As there were reasonably stable conditions of temperature (at about 40°F. (4.4°C.)) and atmosphere in the vaults, variable factors were sought which might have had some influence on adipocere formation: these may be summarised. Adipocere was found in 62.2 per cent of the female remains, but in only 45.4 per cent of the male. A slightly higher incidence of adipocere was present in the remains of those who died in the second and third quarters of the year, when the atmospheric temperature was higher than in the remaining six months of each year, while ambient temperatures at or below freezing point during the pre-inhumation periods were associated with a reduction in the incidence of adipocere. Fog or haze during the pre-inhumation period, regardless of the temperature at the time, were associated with a higher rate of adipocere. No association was apparent between the occurrence of adipocere and the age at death, the length of the pre-inhumation period, or the rainfall during this period.

The early postmortem hydrolysis of fat has already been discussed (see page 5) where it was pointed out that the process commences under the influence of intrinsic lipases, thereafter continuing in the presence of bacterial enzymes, especially those of the Clostridia group. The water required for the hydrolysis is derived mainly from the body tissues, which consequently become more and more dehydrated.

When the change takes place in a body immersed in water this fluid obviously contributes to the hydrolysis of the subcutaneous fat, but the formation of adipocere in deeper sites proceeds before the extraneous water gains access to the interior of the body cavities.

THE DISTRIBUTION OF ADIPOCERE

It is interesting to reflect that until comparatively recently, the prevailing view was that adipocere was a change confined to the subcutaneous regions, yet the occurrence of adipocere in all parts of the body formerly occupied by adipose tissues had been seen by Fourcroy and carefully detailed by Ure in 1831. The description of the typical adipocerous body given by the latter author still remains worthy of study, and it has been amply confirmed that adipocere can form in any site where fatty tissue or fat was present before death, the more obviously affected tissues being those of the subcutaneous, retroperitoneal and mesenteric regions.

Smaller aggregations of fat are also converted to adipocere and may thus become accentuated as the increase in bulk which accompanies adipocere formation is particularly evident in these restricted sites: thus retro-orbital adipocere, formed from the fat within the bony orbit, may cause the eye to be thrust forward so that despite drying and collapse of the globe, the anterior surface of the eye assumes a convexity deceptively like that of a fresh eye. Thymic fat is similarly altered, and the size of the thymus when assessed from the bulk of its adipocere may seem to be unduly great.

After a considerable period of time the only gross indication of the kidneys is more often than not the adipocere which formed from the pelvic fat of these organs. The fat of the bone marrow is often converted to adipocere (Evans, 1962(I)) though not infrequently the medullary cavity of bones is found to be more or less empty. Fatty tissue which is not particularly evident on gross examination, such as that included between the fibres of skeletal muscle and in the myocardium, also participates in the production of adipocere: occasionally the whitish-gray streaks of adipocere can be discerned in the dehydrated, shrunken muscle, but often the detection of adipocere in these situations is achieved only by microscopy.

Adipocere has also been found, again usually on microscopic examination, in the substance of the liver and the kidneys, where visible fat is not normally apparent during life (Evans, 1962(II)). It is virtually certain that in these cases a degree of pathological fatty accumulation had been present before death, and the occasional finding of large masses of adipocere in the myocardium must similarly indicate an antemortem fatty condition in that muscle.

CHANGES IN NON-ADIPOCEROUS TISSUES

When adipocere is widespread, the soft tissues of the body are remarkably dry unless there has been prolonged immersion in water, though even then regions of dehydration may be observed. The extent to which tissues and organs can be recognised in the dry adipocerous body depends upon the amount of tissue protein which was destroyed in the early stages of simple decomposition, and upon the degree to which stromal tissues were damaged by invading larvae, beetles and the like, after adipocere formation had commenced. There is also the difficulty which attends anatomical dissection of retracted, collapsed and hardened tissues.

Often the anterior wall of the abdomen can become so scaphoid that it approaches very near to the posterior wall, the shrivelled surviving abdominal organs becoming thinly sandwiched between these inelastic muscular and adipocerous layers. The intestines and lungs are commonly parchment-like in consistency and thinness, and hearts are reduced to 40g. or less. The most prominent abdominal organ is usually the liver which is apt to retain its shape though its weight is perhaps halved.

As would be expected from the early disappearance of lymphoid tissue during decomposition, the identification of the spleen from any of its persisting fibro-muscular stroma is extremely difficult and lymph nodes have not been made out in these bodies.

SUPERFICIAL PIGMENTATION

The epidermis vanishes as adipocere forms, presumably from a combination of decomposition and shedding, and the dermis becomes darkened in bodies interred in coffins, shades of brown and occasionally black appearing. The nature of these pigments has not yet been determined. Egyptian mummies commonly exhibit comparable pigmentation, and the experimental application of artificially-made natron (which is very alkaline), produces a dark brown colour of the surface of postmortem skin and accelerates the loss of the epidermis.

A dark orange-brown colour can be generated on moist freshly-dead skin by the action of nitrous fumes followed by ammonia gas, at concentrations well above those likely to be present in a sealed coffin; this sequence recalls the xanthoproteic reaction and it has been supposed by Krefft to be partly responsible for alterations in the hair keratin of inhumed bodies. Krefft made no reference to the pigmentary changes in the skin. It is very doubtful that such a chemical reaction does indeed occur spontaneously in the dead body to the extent necessary to cause the observed discolouration of the skin: more probably the foundations for the colour changes are laid by the chemical alterations of tissues and pigments in the skin during early decomposition.

The possibility that the surface browning and blackening of adipocerous bodies in wooden coffins might be due in some way to the proximity of damp wood has been considered. Tissues become brown on prolonged contact with decomposing wood, especially when soil and rotting soil-debris are present and have formed humus, and this may well account for some of the colour seen on coffined bodies exhumed from earth burials after the coffin boards have rotted and the humus-like material has closely surrounded the remains. This cannot be the explanation of the pigmentation found in bodies inhumed in relatively dry environments, as any decay in the coffin wood is of a dry nature, and dry coffin-lining material and shroud or clothing, free from brown discolouration, separates the integument from the wood.

Browning and sometimes blackening is also a feature of the nails in these cases, and a certain amount of darkening of hair is seen. The latter, which is often only slight, seems almost certainly to be due to absorption of soluble pigments formed during the decomposition of other tissues, and the colouring of the nails may prove to be of this nature.

Skin may darken after death from the action of sunlight or of ultraviolet light in the 3000 to 4200Å range, which intensifies melanin pigmentation (Armstrong *et al.*). This postmortem suntan, the Meirowsky phenomenon, is unrelated to spontaneous intrinsic changes, and, like the comparable process in living skin, it causes darkening only in those regions exposed to the light: such a reaction cannot take place in an enclosed coffin. A similar postmortem darkening of the skin is caused by moderately prolonged heating, the result being seen in one to three days at 56°C., but, again, this heating does not occur in normal inhumations.

A common feature of the skin of adipocerous bodies is the presence of numerous whitish-gray rounded excrescences, varying from 1 mm to 1 cm in diameter and superficially resembling moulds: they are, in fact, protruding clusters of acicular crystals from the underlying adipocere.

MUSCLE PIGMENTATION

The skeletal muscles of these bodies merit a special note. Small muscles are dehydrated to wafer thinness and may be inconspicuous in the layers of adipocere; they have a uniform greyish colour. The surface of larger muscles is also gray and the exact line of demarcation between the muscle and adjacent adipocere can be very difficult to ascertain. When adipocere formation is incomplete, as in a body dead for months rather than years, the deeper parts of bulky muscles such as those of the upper parts of the limbs, the longissimus and sacrospinal muscles, the glutei and the psoas, retain a moist redness. The colour is due mostly to myohaemoglobin and it is relatively stable in air: it is the only gross indication of the recent nature of the adipocerous change.

In bodies with complete conversion of the fat to adipocere, a pink-to-red colour is present in the depths of large muscles and it is occasionally, though not often, seen throughout some muscles. This pigment differs from that in the fresher muscle: the tissue is dry and the colour less intense, and it gradually fades on exposure to the atmosphere, although the fading is generally slow and up to forty-eight hours can elapse before the exposed cut surface is quite gray. In a few instances the reddish colour seen immediately on cutting into a muscle has been bright enough to give the impression of muscle freshly dead, even though the death occurred more than 100 years previously.

A red colour in the muscles of bodies dead for some time has been noted before, and an extreme example is found in the account of Tolmachoff in 1929 of the dissection of a Siberian mammoth disinterred after lying for many thousand of years in icy surroundings. The muscle was described as bright red and the fat white or yellow, but there is no mention of adipocere and this may be an example of preservation by cooling alone. The perceptive Collignon, in his account of the exhumation of a human body to which reference has been made (see page 42), mentioned a red colour in a psoas muscle after the body had been buried for more than 200 years, other muscles being a dark brown: he omitted to say whether the colour was stable or not, and the presence of adipocere is inferred and not stated. It may also be recalled that Mansfield noted that the deeper tissues of the lower part of a body recovered from water resembled boiled ham (see page 46), and there was almost certainly adipocere in these remains.

More recently, attention has been drawn by Camps to the occurrence of a pink colour of muscle in association with adipocere. In the course of investigations of a multiple

murder in London, the body of a woman aged nineteen
years was exhumed after burial in a coffin in a cemetery for
some three years: with this body was also the body of her
fourteen months old child, the smaller body lying in the
same coffin on top of the mother's body. Adipocere had
formed in both bodies. A pink colour was seen on that part
of the surface of the woman's body upon which the body of
the child had lain, and the colour disappeared on exposure
to air. Muscle from the woman's thigh was pink, but there
was very little pigmentation in muscle from the child.

The pink pigment in the muscle could not be extracted
with water, and so lung tissues, which were also pink and
likewise faded in the air, were examined spectroscopically as
squash preparations. The absorption bands obtained in this
way were in keeping with the pigment being a haem compound. The possibility of this being carboxyhaemoglobin
had to be considered, but no confirmatory absorption bands
were detected. A diffuse, bright pink colour was seen on the
crowns of the teeth in the jaws of the exhumed woman. This
was not due to carboxyhaemoglobin, and it, too, was thought
probably to be a haem compound, and it could well have
been that as a consequence of strangulation, there had been
haemorrhages into the dental pulp which accentuated the
quantity of haemoglobin present in the teeth at the time of
death.

No red colouration of the teeth has been seen in the
numbers of adipocerous bodies personally examined; at the
most there was a very superficial brown to dark-brown staining of the exposed surface of the enamel, but none of these
bodies showed any indication of death by strangulation.

The pink or red colour personally seen in the dry muscles
of bodies in which adipocere was established has been personally investigated in collaboration with Swale. It was
found that the fading of the colour was prevented by storing
pieces of the muscle in pure nitrogen, and the colour was
restored by this means in samples of muscle which had been

seen to fade from pink to gray. The colour did not develop in muscles in which no pinkish hue had been apparent at any time previously, and they remained uniformly gray. Spectroscopic investigations of aqueous extracts of the pigment showed absorption peaks which strongly suggested that the pigment was of the nature of pent-dio-pent, a derivative of haemoglobin or myohaemoglobin.

The storage of initially-fresh, blood-containing tissues at low temperatures in the presence of atmospheric oxygen leads to the slow formation of methaemoglobin. Such a compound would not be expected to form in inhumed bodies, and no trace of it has been detected in adipocerous tissues.

ADIPOCERE FORMATION IN WATER

When a body in which adipocere developed during submersion remains in fresh or salty water, the surviving stromal tissues, with the exception of the hard tissues and, in a few instances, the brain, ultimately become saturated and the adipocere is wet and soggy. Much mechanical damage may result from water craft, animals and birds, and, in tidal or flowing waters, from hard objects under the water and a good deal of the body may be destroyed. The ligaments are liable to decay and limbs tend to become detached until finally little of the body remains intact. In such circumstances, it may be difficult to assess the quantum of destructive change due to putrefaction alone, and the degree of adipocerous change may seem to be slight.

Examination and dissection of the soaked body are facilitated if the remains are allowed to dry, preferably in the cold, when the adipocere develops a firm consistency and a characteristic colour, and the stromal tissues assume a harder and more easily recognisable condition. The impression has been gained that bodies recovered from the water dry more rapidly if extensive adipocere is present than if the adipose tissues contain much neutral fat, but this point remains to be proved. An undoubted advantage of allowing sodden adipocerous remains to dry is that this simple change of state noticeably reduces the odour of the remains.

CHARACTERISTICS OF ADIPOCERE

Fully developed adipocere is a mixture of fatty acids with some soaps. Palmitic acid is the main constituent of human adipocere and, according to Rutter *et al.* (cited by Mant, 1957), hydrostearic acids, stearic acids and oleic acid account for the remainder of the fatty acid content. The physico-chemical characteristics are such as would be expected of the mixture: the adipocere is firm or hard when cold, and softer and greasy at room temperature. On warming, the greater part of the substance melts, to set again on cooling. Adipocere when dry has a grayish-white colour, but it can absorb pigments and become darkened; dried adipocere has a tendency to crumble slowly when it is immersed in fluid. The substance fluoresces in ultra-violet light, usually with a white to purple colour, but occasionally tints of violet have been seen.

A high percentage of the constituents of adipocere are extracted by hot petroleum ether or hot ethanol: the proportion of the ether-soluble fraction, determined by extraction in a Sohxlet apparatus, has been found to vary from about 50 per cent to 95 per cent in samples of adipocere taken from different bodies after comparable periods of inhumation, and a variation has been noted in samples of adipocere from different anatomical sites in single bodies. An important cause of this seemingly wide range of variation in composition appears to be the quantity of connective tissue of non-lipid nature which has been unavoidably incorporated with the sample of adipocere analysed, and it is this connective tissue which forms very nearly the whole of the insoluble residue after Sohxlet extraction. In the early formative stage of adipocere neutral fat can be detected together with the fatty acids, and the amount of fat diminishes as the adipocere develops, until no neutral fat can be found. The percentage of fatty acids present will not alone indicate the degree to which the adipocere has developed, as quite low figures (e.g., 50%) for the fatty acids can be associated with the complete disappearance of neutral fat (vide supra).

The fatty acids are slowly extracted from adipocere at room temperature by ethanol or chloroform, but after fixation in either Heidenhain's "Susa" or in formol-saline, dehydration of the substance by alcohols of ascending concentration (for histological processing) does not remove all the fatty acids, and clusters of needle-like crystals remain in the tissues and are visible in histological sections cut from paraffin wax blocks (Hunt). Prior fixation with Carnoy's fluid for twenty-four to forty-eight hours leads to the complete disappearance of the crystals (Evans(II)).

A light-brown colour appears in the formol-saline during the period of fixation and the alcohols subsequently used become similarly discoloured. A much more pronounced depth of brown colouration rapidly develops in Carnoy's fluid during the fixation of adipocerous tissues, the pigment being leached out from the proteinous tissues which are included within the adipocere itself.

The crystals seen in histological sections of adipocere are anisotropic and may take up either haematoxylin or eosin. Staining with Sudan IV produces a reddish-brown colour, and a green colour is obtained with the copper-acetate-fluorochrome technique for fatty acids.

There is a divergence of published opinion concerning the odour of adipocere, and it has been described by various authors as intolerable and ammoniacal (Mitchell), very strong (Macleod), fishy like red herring (Manson), ammoniacal with cheesy and earthy taints (Dalton), faecal (Wetherill) and faintly mouldy and cheesy (Glaister) to quote but a few. It is, of course, difficult to liken a strange odour to that of something familiar and the sense of smell is easily fatigued and blunted. Add to these facts the variation of the smell of adipocere according to its age, dryness and temperature, and the difficulty attendant upon the naming of the smell of adipocere can be understood.

Chapter Seven

SPONTANEOUS AND ARTIFICIAL INHIBITION OF POSTMORTEM CHANGES: MUMMIFICATION

IT MUST have been realized long ago that after death a body might putrefy quickly or slowly according to the environmetal circumstances, until little remained but bones, teeth, hair and nails; or else, in desiccating surroundings, that the body might dry out and become a hard, shrivelled, but recognisable object—a natural mummy. The seemingly imputrescible state of a spontaneously-dehydrated corpse must anciently have appealed to mankind, conscious of its physical transience on earth, as a means of ensuring existence for evermore; a desirable quality both for the immediate individual and for revered relatives and elders, and the development of artificial means of preserving bodies would have been a natural consequence.

There is ample evidence that ancient man was aware of bodily changes after death, and that he became able to reproduce some of the natural processes which prevent or retard decay. The drying of bodies by burial in hot dry sand would serve several purposes at once: the body is conveniently out of the way though still easily accessible at any time, it is reasonably protected from the destructive effects of a number of necrophagous creatures, and it is likely to become sufficiently dehydrated to endure without too much deterioration for a satisfactory space of time. From this simple procedure it could be a not-too-difficult step to the hastening of the drying-out process by means of fire or else by some physico-chemical methods.

It is easy to see how such practices became inextricably entangled with abstract ideas and rationalisations, so that the scientific aspects of the whole business were, at the best, obscured.

Inhumations seem to have been common in Europe in the Bronze Age, but cremations are known. Some cremations were only partial, which suggests that the artificial drying of bodies by fire may have been practiced, occasional technical lapses resulting in a greater or lesser destruction of the body by burning: on the other hand deliberate attempts at cremation may have been made without the total destruction of the remains always being achieved (see page 85).

EGYPTIAN METHOD

Burial in sand or in the sandy gravel and limestone detritus of the desert was practiced in predynastic Egypt, and skeletal remains and fragments of skin have been found in interments made at least as long ago as about 4,000 B.C. Bodies inhumed in constructed tombs succumbed to natural decay: this undesirable state of affairs was remedied by the development of artificial mummification. Remains from the earliest dynasties indicate that simple attempts to preserve bodies artificially had been made during that period; wrapping with bandages and some superficial applications of various substances appear to have been the chief methods used (Emery).

Quite possibly the techniques of artificial mummification developed very slowly at first, and until a fairly reliable process was evolved and a sufficiency of trained technicians recruited, probably relatively few bodies were treated. The evidence points to the restriction of the preservative methods at first to the bodies of those deemed to have been of importance during life.

The development of artificial mummification progressed from a simple external treatment of the body to much more elaborate methods which included the separate processing of internal organs.

Two means were adopted for dealing with the viscera: in one, oil was introduced into the anus which was then plugged before the outside of the body was treated, while in the other fairly complete evisceration was performed and the organs and the carcass were attended to separately. Doubtless, observations of bodies putrefying in a hot climate had soon led to the discovery that much of the destructive change commenced in the internal organs.

Eventually, mummification by artificial processes became a highly stylised routine in Egypt. In the more elaborate methods, the body was washed in water from the Nile (for this was the source of life to the Egyptians), the brain was hooked out and the trunk eviscerated in such a manner as to leave the heart and, sometimes, the kidneys in situ. The removed organs were preserved and wrapped up either for their eventual return to the body cavity or else for storage in canopic jars. Meanwhile the body was cleaned and treated with brine or natron, which is an alkaline mixture of sodium salts, the latter being applied either dry or made up with water. The body cavity was washed and treated with aromatic substances and the external applications were then washed off and the body dried.

A number of substances were used at different times for the subsequent preparation of the dried body, varying from the simple application of hot bitumen or hot resin, to more elegant ointments and oils. The hot applications sealed the surface of the body but were damaging to the tissues. It was this practice, which seems to have been a later modification, which gave rise to the word "mummy," from the Persian "mummiai" meaning pitch. The aromatic ointments and oils, which sometimes included animal fat, enhanced the appearance of the skin and must have greatly improved the odour.

In the less complex process in which evisceration was not performed, it became important to remove or to destroy the contents of the bowel, and this was the reason for the introduction and retention of cedar or similar oil per anum while the superficial applications were made to the body. When this external process was complete, and this was customarily deemed to require seventy days, the oil was allowed to run out. It is likely that the oil had little appreciable effect on the intestinal contents or on the abdominal organs, but it would serve as a convenient vehicle for the ultimate removal of much of the tissues which had become liquefied by decomposition. A summary of the techniques of artificial mummification in Egypt has been made by Rowling.

The numerous accounts of examinations of Egyptian mummies make it clear that the degree of preservation did not achieve a very high standard, and it seems a pity that the elaborate, lengthy and doubtless costly process did not produce better or more permanent results. To be sure, in many cases some facial details have been apparent, but on the whole the Egyptian mummy is apt to be anatomically disappointing. The integument and muscles are usually dry and very brittle and the bones, especially the ribs, may be similarly affected so that in some cases little disturbance of the remains is required to cause the body to crumble and collapse within its wrappings, literally becoming as dust. In other cases, however, the outer tissues have remained harder and have become almost impossible to cut without some flaking, cracking and breaking occurring, though it has occasionally been possible to cut and trim blocks of these tissues for histological processing without undue loss of the tissue.

Fundamentally, the ancient method of mummification in Egypt, as in other countries, produced dehydration of the body, partly by the removal of viscera which permitted evaporation to dry out the body cavity, and partly by the mixtures of hydrophilic salts which were applied internally and externally. Common salt (which was used as brine, as a solid, and mixed with natron) dehydrates tissues quite satisfactorily provided that the salt can penetrate into the deeper layers of the tissues; this was probably achieved well enough by rubbing the salt into the tissues and by the lengthy time during which the salt was kept in contact with the tissues.

Natron alone also removes water from tissues but it has a far greater damaging effect than salt, and personally-conducted laboratory experiments have shown that a mixture of salts corresponding to the analysis of natron given by Lucas causes browning of the epidermis within a few hours after application to the skin of a freshly dead body, and the epidermis is gradually loosened so that after a few days it can be peeled off from the dermis with ease. Similar results are obtained when mixtures of artificial natron and salt are used. This damaging effect was known to the Egyptians who made provisions for the collection and storage of the shed epidermis, and it probably accounts for the fact that in many cases the head and neck were not treated with natron.

During the process of artificial mummification, as in the development of spontaneous mummification, some of the intrinsic water in the tissues is utilised in the natural hydrolysis of the fat in the adipose tissues. Fatty acids rather than neutral fat are found to predominate in the adipose regions of mummies, whether mummification had been achieved by spontaneous or by artificial means, though the extent to which fatty acids form and persist depends upon the rapidity with which dehydration is brought about and on the operation of oxidative changes (see pages 6 & 73). The production of these fatty acids is all the more likely to take place when the superficial tissues have been steeped in alkaline mixtures such as natron.

Applications of various ointments and oils also formed part of the process of artificial mummification, and the substances used included gum-resins, resins and wood oils

(Lucas). Such substances were almost certainly more effective cosmetically than as preservatives. It is true that these natural products have a slight bactericidal effect, but no convincing proof of their value as inhibitors of the decomposition of skin has been obtained from laboratory experiments, and applications of animal fat to dead skin seem more to hasten rather than to retard decomposition of the skin. Inunction of these substances into dried and dehydrated skin improves the appearance and increases the flexibility of the tissues: they also tend to exclude air and moisture, and thus, to a slight extent, their application serves to protect the tissues.

Encasing mummified bodies in a hard impervious shell, produced by applying hot bitumen and similar substances, was thought at one time to be an excellent way of protecting the remains against deterioration. In fact the process itself caused a good deal of damage, for the tissues were badly charred by the heat of the applications. As the destructive thermal effects were hidden by the coating of bituminous substances, it is quite possible that the embalmers were quite unaware of this defect of their technique.

EXAMINATION OF MUMMIFIED TISSUES

The changes brought about in the tissues by the various mummifying techniques have been studied in the gross and histologically. The latter offers some opportunities for noting the survival of different tissues and any modifications of the normal histo-chemistry; the more searching methods of electron microscopy have also been brought to bear on mummy tissues.

The physical state of the tissues creates difficulties in the initial preparations for histological sectioning: whether the tissue be in large pieces, or in small flakes almost down to dust-particle size, the hardness and brittle quality has necessitated the use of softening agents. In none of the mummy tissues handled personally has it been possible to produce satisfactory histological sections unless preliminary softening had been attained. The hard and seemingly durable state of the tissues might lead to the impression that the protein had become insoluble and "fixed" in the histological sense: this is not so and it is necessary to fix the tissues as well as softening them as part of the histological processing, otherwise the sections distintegrate in the staining and other solutions.

Several softening agents have personally been tried on mummy tissues, and three methods found to produce satisfactory results are: soaking blocks trimmed as small as safety permits in N-saline for periods up to seven days followed by 2 per cent aqueous formaldehyde for seven days; soaking the block in buffered 2 per cent aqueous formaldehyde for seven to twenty-one days; steeping the block in 1 per cent potassium hydroxide for forty-eight hours.

Softening processes used by others include 1 to 3 per cent potassium hydroxide for twelve to forty-eight hours until the tissue swells, then 3 per cent formaldehyde (Wilder): 2 per cent sodium carbonate with 0.5 per cent formaldehyde for twenty-four hours (Ruffer): 1 to 2 per cent formaldehyde (Williams): 1.2 per cent saline then 4 per cent formaldehyde for twenty-four to forty-eight hours, or equal parts of glycerine and 10 per cent acetic acid for twenty-four to forty-eight hours (Graf).

A more extended programme has been put forward by Sandison, who recommends a mixture of 96 per cent ethanol 30 vols., 1 per cent aqueous formaldehyde 50 vols., 5 per cent aqueous sodium carbonate 20 vols. When the tissue has become jelly-like it is transferred to a solution containing 2/3rds of the mixture and 1/3rd 96% ethanol, and this is replaced by further quantities of the solution until the tissue is firm. Sandison has also employed mollifex (British Drug Houses) and a softening fluid of Flatters and Garnet. For the preparation of material for electron microscopy, Leeson used the softening mixture developed by Sandison.

The softening agents personally tested bring about swelling of the tissues, evidently from a degree of re-hydration. When the process has been allowed to continue beyond the limits normally desired for histological work, it has been seen that the initially hard tissue becomes more and more swollen and pulpy until it begins to break up: it has not been found to dissolve. The steeping fluid becomes brown to dark brown and the tissue correspondingly a little lighter in colour. Smears from the disintegrating tissue have failed to demonstrate recognisable cells, and it does not appear that softening simply causes cellular elements to become detached as clumps of cells or individual cells, such as might happen if the cells had survived and the intercellular cement had been altered by the solutions, becoming either less adhesive or else destroyed. It has also not been possible to detect separated individual cells by the use of hyaluronidase.

The further process used personally for histological preparation consists of fixing the softened tissue in 10 per cent formol-saline for two to seven days, dehydrating slowly in alcohols of ascending concentration, clearing in xylene, benzene or chloroform, then double-embedding in colloidon and paraffin wax (M.P. 57°C.). Sandison has found modifications to this phase of processing to be helpful, including passage through 8 per cent phenol in 96 per cent ethanol and amyl acetate.

THE SURVIVAL OF MUMMIFIED TISSUES

The tissues usually demonstrable by histological investigations of mummified material are collagen, elastic tissue (mostly in the media of blood-vessels), cardiac and skeletal muscle, cartilage and bone: these tissues usually respond to "special" methods of staining, giving tinctorial results similar to those from "recent" tissues. It is noteworthy that the transverse striations of muscle have been demonstrated by several investigators including Sandison, Williams and Ruffer, though Graf commented on the absence of striations in the muscle from his Egyptian material. Reticulin is described by Shaw in his account of the remains of Har Mose. The axis cylinders of nerves seem not to survive intact in ancient mummies, only amorphous material remaining, but the course of nerves has sometimes been limned by their surviving nerve sheaths (Shaw; Williams; Graf).

The question whether nuclei persist in these mummified tissues is not completely answered as yet: Ruffer describes nuclei in Egyptian material; Shaw and Williams both mention the absence of nuclei in Egyptian and Peruvian mummy tissues, while Rowling notes the rarity of nuclei in his specimens. Nuclei have not been recognised in the mummy material examined personally, and in this and other respects a close similarity has been found in the histological appearances of mummified and of adipocerous tissues.

The advent of electron microscopy into this field of research has resulted in the discovery of cell membranes, nuclear membranes and chromatin in American Indian mummy tissue according to Leeson. The persistence of cell details, including nuclei, clearly requires further investigation, and the continued use of electron microscopy may go far in resolving the problem.

Another difficulty, though perhaps of lesser complexity, concerns the survival of erythrocytes, and again there is a lack of unanimity in the published observations as to whether or not these cells are to be found in mummy tissues. Erythrocytes were seen in such tissues by Sandison and Graf, the latter finding them in Egyptian mummy tissues from which the walls of the blood-vessels had vanished, and, together with other cells, in bone marrow from Swedish skeletons, though the identity of the cells is admittedly queried. The possible presence of red cells in the marrow cavity of ancient bone has also been noted by Moodie, who noticed structures which he thought might have been fossilised erythrocytes in dinosaur bones, though of course, these remains were not mummified. Rowling found that erythrocytes were seldom present in the Egyptian material he examined: Shaw identified blood-vessels and found them to be well defined and with elastic laminae, but they were either empty or contained only granular or hyaline substance, no red cells being identified. Williams saw red cells in only one area, thought possibly to be a haemorrhage, in his Peruvian specimens, and in this case some filaments were associated with the cells. Some iron was also present, but this could have been derived from the soil.

Objects resembling erythrocytes have personally been seen in mummy tissues, but so far they have always been shown by morphological and staining characteristics to be fungal spores, sometimes but not always associated with filaments; no undoubted erythrocytes have been found in these tissues.

Connective tissues, then, form virtually the whole of the substance of mummified remains, the stromal material of bone, cartilage, collagen, reticulin and muscle enduring with scarcely any modification save dehydration and, with the exception of bone, shrinkage.

MUMMIFICATION AND ADIPOCERE

The tissues of a natural mummy closely resemble those of the prepared mummy, and it has long been assumed that the only spontaneous process which brings about natural mummification is simple dehydration by evaporation. Undoubtedly, mummification occurs most readily when conditions favour evaporation, as when a steady current of warm dry air passes across a body for some time, but the external environment may not be the only factor concerned in the production of a mummy.

The discovery of fatty acids in the subcutaneous regions of natural and prepared mummies shows that some hydrolysis of neutral fat has occurred in these bodies, and there can be little doubt that adipocere has formed in some of these cases. The dry and dehydrated nature of the non-fatty tissues of adipocerous bodies compares with that of the same tissues in mummies, and the differentiation between mummification and adipocere formation can be less easily made than has been implied in the past.

In a drying environment (as distinct from a dry one), some hydrolysis of fat occurs and this is partly responsible for the dehydration of the non-fatty tissues, but the continuing and relatively rapid loss of water by evaporation halts hydrolysis before it has reached completion: oxidative changes in the fat and the fatty acids may then become quite marked in this type of environment. In contrast, in an enclosed dry environment such as a sound coffin, virtually no water will be lost from the body by evaporation and the complete hydrolysis of fat will therefore be favoured, while the intensely reducing conditions which develop will arrest any oxidative changes.

Thus, whether the retardation of decomposition of a body will be brought about by spontaneous "classical" mummification or by adipocere formation is likely to depend not only upon simple drying, but upon the rate of drying and the extent to which external factors influence the drying, as well as the oxidising or reducing nature of the immediate ambient, and the initial amount of neutral fat in the remains.

Chapter Eight

FACTORS WHICH INHIBIT
POSTMORTEM CHANGES

RETARDATION OF EARLY CHANGES

M ETHODS for the artificial preservation of animal tissues were developed and practiced in antiquity, and two major objectives were recognized. One was the preservation in a life-like manner of the mortal remains of deceased members of the community or of certain animals of religious or magical importance; the other was so to preserve edible meats that a supply of this food would be available during travels and seasonal shortages of animals suitable for slaughter. An important difference between these two widely removed ends is that in the former the human or animal body was maintained in as complete a form as possible and restored by various means to a semblance of its living state (as in the various forms of mummification), while animal carcases to be saved for eating would be flayed, eviscerated, disjointed, cut up and preserved without much regard for anatomical appearances. Expressed in a different way, the motive in one case was abstract, magical or religious, and in the other strictly material.

There can be little doubt that as the science of food preservation advanced, so the need for ceaseless hunting activities diminished, leaving mankind with more time for cogitation and enquiry into abstract matters.

THE EFFECTS OF EXHAUSTION AND REST

A variety of processes are available for the preservation of uncooked edible animal products, but the first requisite is that decomposition should be retarded as soon after the death of the animal as possible. It has long been known that animals exhausted by the heat of the chase before being wounded and killed pass rapidly into the state of rigor mortis and tend subsequently to decompose more rapidly than those killed swiftly after an adequate rest period. Decomposition is slower, also, if the body of the animal is bled and eviscerated soon after death.

The rested animal has ample glycogen in the muscles which is available for the postmortem production of lactic acid, and if this compound is present in sufficient quantity, it tends to inhibit the growth of bacteria in the tissues and thus it retards the onset of decomposition due to bacterial action. Physical exhaustion depletes the store of glycogen and thereby greatly reduces the postmortem production of lactic acid. The earlier onset of rigor mortis in the exhausted animal is closely bound up with the diminution of glycogen, (see page 32) but it is unlikely that rigor itself affects the rate of decomposition.

SIMPLE COOLING

Evisceration and flaying result in the loss of blood and they hasten the cooling of the carcass and the isolated organs by increasing the surface area open to the air. An element of dehydration is introduced by evaporation from the exposed surfaces. The spread of bacteria from the intestines to other organs is prevented by skilled evisceration, and bleeding removes a medium in which organisms spread throughout the carcase, as well as serving further to reduce the temperature of the tissues. Smaller animals possess a relatively large surface area in relation to body weight, especially after evisceration, consequently cooling is faster and decomposition slower in the small carcase.

PARTIAL PROTEOLYSIS

There are exceptions to the rule that the retardation of decomposition must be attended to immediately after the death of food animals, for certain meats are deemed to be more acceptable when some degree of postmortem change has occurred before cooking. Partial breakdown of the protein of the muscle of game animals improves the flavour, and proteolysis of fibrous connective tissues appreciably softens these otherwise firm and stringy substances. This is particularly the case with venison where the abundant fibrous tissue in the muscles renders it tough until it has been "hung" for a sufficient time. A comparable process applies to the culinary beating of steak, when enzymes liberated from the squashed and disrupted cells hasten proteolysis of the fibrous tissue. Refractory cuts may also be tenderised by the action of additives such as papain and bromelin in "tenderising salt," the added enzyme serving almost as well as the intrinsic enzymes in promoting the required degree of proteolysis.

ANTIBIOTICS

Much of the undesirable change in stored edible meat is a result of postmortem alterations of the tissues brought about by bacterial action, the organisms either having been present in the tissues before death or else appearing as contaminants of the carcase.

So far as the former state is concerned it would be reasonable to assume that the administration of antibiotics fairly shortly before death might, by destroying many of the organisms already present in the animal, delay some of the decomposition and perhaps inhibit a number of the subsequent potential contaminants. This thesis was pursued by Wagner, who treated rats with antibiotics for two days before they were killed, and then exposed the bodies of the animals to a variety of environments and observed the degree of decomposition. The bodies of those rats treated with tetra-

cycline or tetracycline-Ca survived with the least evidence
of postmortem change, and it was asserted that neither exposure to the air nor burial in soil led to appreciable putrefaction up to the 12th day after death. The retardation of
decay was less marked when the antibiotic was either strep-
tomycin, penicillin or sulphathiazole. The results reported
with the tetracyclines are most remarkable and merit further
investigation.

Such a striking inhibition of postmortem change has not
been noticed in the human body for the relatively short
period during which the body is normally available for postmortem observations, and personal studies have led to the
conclusion that more refined investigations than simple in-
spection are necessary before it can be accepted that postmortem changes in the human body are significantly affected
by terminal antibiotic therapy. It must, however, be admitted that usually there is one great difference between a
healthy experimental animal given an antibiotic and then
killed, and a human being to whom the drug is administered
as a therapeutic measure for, in the latter case, death is likely
to be an expression of failure of the control of the infection,
and furthermore the tissues will be already modified before
death by the direct and remote effects of disease.

An alternative way of employing antibiotics to suppress
the contamination of dead tissues, particularly edible meats,
is to apply the antibiotic in some suitable form to the tissues
after death. In this manner there is likely to be suppression
of some, at least, of the bacteria on and very near the exposed
surfaces of the tissues. This partial "sterilisation" may so reduce the bacterial contamination that the changes of decomposition are sufficiently retarded for the storage period of
the tissues to be usefully extended without any further special preservation methods being used.

It has been established that chicken carcases which have
been immersed for two hours in slush ice to which chlortet-
racycline has been added keep in a good condition for a

longer period than similar carcases not treated with the antibiotic (Bate-Smith), while fish treated in this way had a 50 per cent extension of storage "life" (Reay).

SUGAR

A much older and, to a point, a more attractive method of preserving edible meats consists of the direct application of a layer of honey or sugar. The former substance ante-dates the latter, and honey was used in antiquity also for the preservation of human remains, at least for periods of transport from some foreign field to the homeland: the re-mains of Alexander the Great were supposedly treated in this manner. Until relatively recently it was a common cus-tom to preserve meat in honey for winter consumption, though, judging from some of the old accounts, towards the end of the winter the effects of the honey were more valued as a disguise for the taste of the meat than as a lasting pre-servative.

A coating in which there is a high concentration of sugar directly inhibits the growth of superficial fungi and bacteria and further preservative effects are due to a slight degree of dehydration produced in the tissues (sugar, like salt, being hydrophilic) together with the exclusion of light and at-mospheric oxygen.

SMOKING

A degree of surface decontamination combined with de-hydration and chemical modification of tissues can be achieved by exposing them to a suitably high concentration of wood smoke.

The heat which is necessary for the production of the smoke, as well as the heat of the smoke itself has a drying effect on the tissues which is maximal at the exposed sur-faces, and this in turn produces some dehydration of the deeper tissues because of the outward diffusion of water. The extent of the drying is a function of the length of time to which the tissues are exposed to the heat; increases of temperature are more likely to lead to carbonisation of the tissue surfaces, when a hard, almost impervious outer crust will form while the deeper tissues remain moist because evaporation is virtually arrested.

In regulated smoking a film of smoke particles accumulates on the tissues, and amongst other substances there gradually builds up a mixture of phenols, creosol, guaiacol and formaldehyde on the surface. In addition to the inhibitory action this mixture has upon flora, there is also an action upon the tissues whose proteins are gradually precipitated and rendered moderately resistant to rehydration and decomposition. The extent to which the chemical preservation effects penetrate the tissues depends on both the efficiency of the smoking and the nature and thickness of the treated tissues.

COLD

Chemical reactions are generally slowed by cooling, and the complex systems which operate during decomposition are no exception to this rule.

In the course of his investigations into putrefaction, Bacon had established that it was inhibited by cold (Bacon 11), and the furtherance of experiments along this line probably led to his death. Bacon caught a fatal chill after gathering snow for the purpose of packing it in and around a chicken carcase, to see how satisfactory was this means of cooling tissues.

Moderate cooling delays decomposition to an appreciable degree, while "deep" freezing (at less than freezing point) can so retard postmortem changes that tissues may be preserved satisfactorily for long periods of time. The resistance to decay of deeply-frozen dead tissues persists only for as long as the suitably-cold ambient is maintained; unlike prolonged drying, cold does not modify tissues sufficiently to ensure their continued unchanged existence for any length of time at normal temperatures.

Crystals of ice form in tissues as they are cooled to freezing point and below, and the withdrawal of water from the tissues and its immobilisation as ice reduces the fluid content of the cells and interstitial tissues. With reduction of the temperature of the tissues below 0°C. an increasing proportion of the water in the tissues is converted to ice crystals, and this dehydrating effect is most marked during cooling from 5 to 10°C. below freezing (Meryman). Rather more than 90 per cent of tissue water may ultimately form ice, the remainder of the water being prevented from passing into this phase because of its chemical bonding with cellular compounds.

The reduction of the intracellular and extracellular water brought about by freezing diminishes the transfer of soluble substances within and between cells by reducing diffusion, thus inhibiting chemical reactions: further inhibition is due to the direct effects of the cold, particularly upon enzymal reactions.

Moderate rates of cooling induce the formation of large crystals of ice in the extracellular spaces, while rapid freezing produces smaller and more numerous crystals, and intracellular ice crystals now appear.

The development of cellular dehydration due to freezing raises the concentration of intracellular substances, which may damage the cells: with the progress of cellular dehydration, the cells shrink and become distorted. While living cells can withstand this form of trauma and they survive even though freezing may bring about the collapse of their form (Meryman), dead cells with cytoplasmic membranes already impaired by postmortem changes are liable to rupture.

The protein of frozen, and thereby dehydrated, dead cells is apt to be altered by becoming denatured and relatively insoluble: thus when thawing takes place, the water from the melting ice in the tissues is not fully re-absorbed by the protein and so it remains as excess water. A further loss of water occurs on thawing when the cells have been disrupted earlier during the freezing process. When either of these causes of water-loss operate, the thawing tissues become unduly wet and they freely drip fluid which contains crystalloids, proteins, pigments and breakdown products. The more rapidly the tissues are frozen initially, the less will be the fluid loss on thawing. Repeated freezing and thawing increases cellular damage and the ultimate loss of water and soluble substances becomes correspondingly greater.

In normal ambients, dew appears on the surface of thawing tissues and this contributes further to the wetness of the tissues, but it is unlikely that the formation of dew causes any additional loss of tissue constitutents.

Tissues which have been cooled by being in contact with ice rather than by more efficient methods are less well preserved because the temperature of the tissues is likely not to be low enough to prevent them becoming saturated with water: in these circumstances decomposition will occur, though slowly, while the wetness may permit the growth of those fungi which tolerate cold. Such conditions are found in the field, for example, in the winters of temperate climes.

The frozen remains of about thirty-nine mammoths have been discovered at various times (Farrand), and the degree to which they had been spontaneously preserved seems to have depended chiefly upon the efficiency of the natural freezing which had occurred. The majority of these remains were mostly decomposed and only four have been found to be nearly completely preserved. Unfortunately, it is difficult to assess the extent of the postmortem change which had taken place during the frozen phase in a number of these remains, for after discovery, some of the mammoths were exposed to the air and left thus before being fully examined a year or more later. A certain amount of the decomposition may therefore have occurred after disinterment. The dissection of one mammoth (Tolmachoff) revealed the more resistant tissues, skin and hair, as well as fat (which was white or yellow) and muscle which was bright red (see page 57).

In contrast to the poor preservation of tissues brought about by contact with ice alone is the remarkably good degree of preservation achieved by freezing accompanied by drying, for this combination of effects very greatly inhibits decomposition. Remains exposed to extremely cold and arid atmospheres can survive for long periods of time, spontaneous mummification being produced by the combination of the dehydrating tendencies of both freezing and evaporation. Mummified carcases of crab-eater seals in the Antarctic region have been described (Pewe et al.; Claridge), one of the remains having been estimated by the C-14 method to have been dead for 1,600 to 2,600 years. On a less remote plane, the applications of freeze-drying to the storage of biological material for laboratory use may be more familiar.

Chapter Nine

THE EFFECTS OF HEAT ON
POSTMORTEM TISSUES

CREMATION

T HE general composition of the average adult human body with its high water content (around 60%) suggests that incineration of the body to incombustible ash would demand a good deal of heat, a steady supply of air or oxygen and a fairly lengthy period of time; against this, the average body has about 15.4Kg. of fat, as established by the cyclopropane method of Lesser *et al.*, and this fat increases to some extent the flammability of the remains. An adult body of about 160 lb. (73Kg.), cremated in a purpose-built furnace fired by gas, and with recirculation of the hot gases, is destroyed to ash in three-fourths to one hour of steady burning at a temperature around 1,600°F. (870°C.). Obese bodies containing as they do more water as well as more fat, are combusted more slowly, and under the same conditions of cremation, more than ninety minutes may pass before the process is complete. Embalming increases the time required for complete cremation by about thirty minutes.

In England, bodies are usually cremated in coffins made of wood and furnished with wooden fittings. The coffin is introduced into the furnace where it rapidly catches fire, bulges and warps, and the coffin sides may collapse and fall, exposing the remains to the direct effect of the flames. The skin and hair at once scorch, char and burn. Heat coagulation of muscle protein may become evident at this stage, causing the muscles slowly to contract, and there may be a steady divarication of the thighs with gradually developing flexion of the limbs. There is a popular idea that early in the cremation process the heat causes the trunk to flex forwards violently so that the body suddenly "sits up," bursting open the lid of the coffin, but this has not been observed personally, nor has this been described to the author by anyone in attendance at cremations in the London district.

Occasionally there is swelling of the abdomen before the skin and abdominal muscles char and split; the swelling is due to the formation of steam and the expansion of gases in the abdominal contents.

Destruction of the soft tissues gradually exposes parts of the skeleton. The skull is soon devoid of covering, then the bones of the limbs appear, commencing at the extremities of the limbs where they are relatively poorly covered by muscle or fat, and the ribs also become exposed. The small bones of the digits, wrists and ankles remain united by their ligaments for a surprising length of time, maintaining the anatomical relationships even though the hands and feet may fall away from the adjacent long bones.

The abdominal contents burn fairly slowly, and the lungs more slowly still: it has been observed that the brain is specially resistant to complete combustion during cremation of the body. Even when the vault of the skull has broken and fallen away, the brain has been seen as a dark, fused mass with a rather sticky consistency, and the organ may persist in this form for most of the time required for the general destruction of the remains: indeed, in one personally-observed instance the thoracic contents and the brain were recognisable ninety minutes after the cremation had begun.

Eventually the spine becomes visible as the viscera disappear, the bones glow whitely in the flames and the skeleton falls apart. Some bones fragment into pieces of various sizes while other bones remain whole.

The usual practice consists of raking out the hot ashes as soon as combustion is complete, in order that the next coffin may be introduced into the furnace without undue loss of heat. There may be sufficient heat remaining for a complete cremation to be performed after the supply of gas has been turned off, the hot gases and the radiant heat from the furnace lining sufficing, with the air draught, to burn the remains.

The ashes are cooled and then crushed in a simple machine to a coarse white powder, the weight of the powder being usually 3 to 4 lb. (some 1.6Kg.), though the incomplete combustion of a large body can produce up to 8 lb. (some 3.6Kg.) of ash.

Before the introduction of purpose-made cremation furnaces, incineration of bodies was carried out by several methods, of which the funeral pyre is a well-known example. This required a large stack of wood which was usually piled pyramidal fashion with the body at the apex. Inflammable oils were often poured onto the pyre, but there was no certainty that these preparations would eventually achieve complete cremation of the remains.

INCOMPLETE COMBUSTION

The likelihood of a cremation being incomplete exists also when bodies are burned by accident or design in blazing premises, and in these circumstances the body is commonly only partially destroyed. Exposed parts of the body will be burned, but parts protected by contact with some surface (or with some other region of the body) may be scarcely more than charred because they are protected from direct heat, and because the contact also causes a local lack of oxygen which inhibits combustion. A similar resistance to burning is seen when sheets of paper are held closely together and exposed to fire: the individual pages of a book blaze readily, but the closed book hardly burns at all. Fires involving highly inflammable substances such as oils are apt to be very destructive to the soft tissues of the body, though when petrol is concerned there may be more of an explosive effect than a quiet burning, with only very superficial destructive changes of the body. Where special circumstances operate to maintain a good supply of air to premises on fire, then the cremation of a body can proceed more or less to completion.

When a body has been heated and only partially combusted a number of characteristic changes may be found. The keratin of hair shafts becomes fused at the distal ends of the hairs, so that there are dark-brown to black swellings, frequently containing a number of minute air bubbles, in the terminations of the hairs (Evans, 1954). The skin also becomes altered with heating. Moderate heat applied to dead skin causes browning and blackening of the epidermis, and steam is produced in the dermal tissues which leads to the production of local swellings as the thin overlying tissues are forced outwards. When the heat is no longer applied further steam production ceases and the steam already present in the dermis reverts to water: the loss of volume inherent in this change brings about the collapse of the "blister."

These effects of heat on dead skin are in sharp contrast to those which occur in living skin when it is similarly heated, for in addition to the damaging effects of the heat there also occur the changes due to acute inflammation, amongst which are a locally-increased vascularity and a serous exudate rich in serum crystalloids and colloids. This exudate is the chief factor in the production of antemortem burn blisters: hence the blisters remain tense and their contents include serum proteins.

With more severe burning there is irreversible coagulation of the dermal proteins, which thus become hardened, and this is seen as a result of burns during life as well as in post-mortem burns. Heat-coagulated collagen and other proteins similarly rendered insoluble are less liable to the changes of postmortem decomposition, for the tissues have become "fixed" and chemically altered. The histo-chemical reactions of such modified tissues also change, and the usual specific stains for the tissues no longer give the normal results. Haemoglobin in the heated tissue tends to break down to haematin.

Severe heating of skin leads to carbonisation of the super-ficial tissues and coagulation of the deeper tissues, including the larger muscles. If this be an extensive change, as in a partly cremated body, then sufficient coagulation of muscle protein can take place to cause pronounced shortening of the muscle fibres and thus bring the limbs to positions of fixed flexion. This result, the postmortem "pugilistic atti-tude," is characteristic of cremation which has been halted before completion, and it is much more striking than the relatively slight shortening of the large muscles which is seen in bodies in the process of being completely combusted in a cremation furnace. In the latter case the muscles are destroyed partially or wholly before the full effects of heat contraction can develop.

REFERENCES

Airth, R. L. and Foester, G. E.: Some aspects of fungal bioluminescence. *J. Cell. Comp. Physiol., 56*(3):173, 1960.

Armstrong, J. A., Fryer, D. I., Stewart, W. K. and Whittingham, H. E.: Interpretation of injuries in the Comet aircraft disasters. *Lancet, 268*(1):1135, 1955.

Bacon, F. (Lord Verulam.) (1): *Sylva Sylvarum or a Natural History in Ten Centuries,* Rawley, W., 1669, *Century IV,* p. 73, ch. 329.

Ibid. (II): *Century IV,* p. 74, ch. 335.

Ibid. (III): *Century IV,* p. 76, ch. 347. Also *Century VIII,* p. 162, ch. 771.

Ibid. (IV): *Century IV,* p. 73, ch. 330.

Ibid. (V): *Century IX,* p. 192, ch. 891.

Ibid. (VI): *Century VII,* p. 139, ch. 678.

Ibid. (VII): *Century IV,* p. 76, ch. 352.

Barral, E.: Formation rapide de gras de cadavre dans la putrefaction cadaverique. *Ann. Méd. lég.,* 7:597, 1927.

Bate-Smith, E. C.: *Food Investigation.* Department of Scientific and Industrial Research, H. M. Stationery Office, London, 1956. p. 39,

Battiscombe, C. F.: *The Relics of St. Cuthbert.* London, Oxford University Press, 1956.

Becker, N. H. and Barron, K. D.: The cytochemistry of anoxia and anoxia-ischaemic encephalopathy in rats. 1. Alterations in neuronal lysosomes identified by acid phosphatase activity. *Am. J. Path., 38*(2):161, 1961.

Berenbom, M., Chang, P. I., Betz, H. E. and Stowell, R. E.: Chemical and enzymatic changes associated with mouse liver necrosis in vitro. *Cancer Res., 15*:1, 1955.

Biancalani, A. and Grassini, R.: Contributo alla conoscenza del-l'adipocera. *Arch. Antrop. Crim.* (4), *50*:1429, 1930.

Biddulph, C., van Fossan, D. D., Criscuolo, D. and Clark, R. T.: Lactic acid concentration of brain tissues of dogs exposed to hypoxemia and/or hypocapnia, *J. Appl. Physiol.*, *13*(3):486, 1958.

Blair, E., Hook, R., Tolley, H. and Bunce, G. E.: Serum glutamic transaminase (GOT) content in hypothermia. *Science, 133*: 105, 1961.

Brit. Med. J. (Annotation): Serum enzymes in myocardial infarction. *1*:566, 1961.

Burstone, M. S. and Miller, F. N.: Histochemical demonstration of changes in cytochrome oxidase activity in human myocardial infarctions. *Am. J. Clin. Path.*, *35*:118, 1961.

Callow, E. H.: *Rigor Mortis, in Food Investigation.* Department of Scientific and Industrial Research, H. M. Stationery Office, London, 1956, p. 31.

Camps, F. E.: *Medical and Scientific Investigations in the Christie Case.* London, Medical Publications Ltd., 1953, p. 53.

Carnot, A.: Recherches sur la composition générale et la teneur en fluor des os modernes et des os fossiles des différents âges. *Ann. Min.*, (Paris), 3:155, 1893.

Claridge, G. G.: Mummified carcasses of crab-eater seals (Lobodon carcinophagus) found in ice-free regions around McMurdo Sound, Ross Dependency, Antarctica. *Nature, 190*:559, 1961.

Collignon, C.: Some account of a body lately found in uncommon preservation under the ruins of the Abbey at St. Edmund's-Bury, Suffolk; with some reflections upon the subject. *Phil. Trans., Roy. Soc., 62*:465, 1772.

Csaszar, Sz. E. and Saucs, O.: Postmortem diagnosis of uraemia. *Keserl-Orvostud, 12*(3):333, 1960 (abstracted in *Excerpta Med.* (Amst.), Sect. V, *14*(5):368, 1961).

Dalton, J. C.: Remarkable case of adipocere. *New York J. Med.,* 7:375, 1859.

Dawkins, M. J. R., Judah, J. D. and Rees, K. R.: Factors influencing the survival of liver cells during autolysis. *J. Path. & Bact.*, 77:257, 1959.

Dominguez, A. M., Halstead, J. R., Chinn, H. I., Goldbaum, L. R., and Lovell, F. W.: Significance of elevated lactic acid in the postmortem brain. *Aerospace Med., 31*:897, 1960.

Emery, W. B.: *Archaic Egypt.* London, Penguin Books, Ltd., 1961, p. 162.

Enticknap, J. B.: Biochemical changes in cadaver sera. *J. Forensic Med., 7*(3):135, 1960.

Enticknap, J. B.: Lipids in cadaver sera after fatal heart attacks. *J. Clin. Path., 14*:496, 1961.

Ernster, L. and Lindberg, O.: Animal mitochondria. *Ann. Rev. Physiol., 20*:13, 1958.

Evans, W. E. D.: in Gradwohl, R. B. H.: *Legal Medicine.* St. Louis, C. V. Mosby Co., 1954, p. 49.

Evans, W. E. D.: Adipocere formation in a relatively dry environment. *Med. Sc. & Law., 3*:145, 1963.

Evans, W. E. D. (I): Adipocere formation in bone, 1962 (in preparation).

Evans, W. E. D. (II): Some histological findings in spontaneously preserved bodies. *Med. Sc. & Law., 2*:155, 1962.

Ezra, H. C. and Cook, S. F.: Amino acids in fossil human bone. *Science, 126*:3263, 1957.

Ezra, H. C. and Cook, S. F.: Histology of mammoth bone. *Science, 129*:465, 1959.

Fallani, M. and Astore, P. A.: Fatty acids of adipose tissue in postmortem transformation. *Minerva Med.-leg.* (Torino), *81*(3-4):116, 1961 (abstracted in *Excerpta Med.* (Amst.), Sect. V, *15*(2):164, 1962).

Farrand, W. R.: Frozen mammoths and modern geology. *Science, 133*:729, 1961.

Gallagher, C. H., Judah, J. D. and Rees, K. R.: Enzymal changes during liver autolysis. *J. Path. Bact., 72*:247, 1956.

Gallo, P.: Biochemical significance of myocardial tissue changes with rigor mortis, under normal conditions and in gamma-hexane poisoning. *Cardiologia, 37,* Suppl. 1, 1960.

Gandy, C. M.: A case of almost complete adipoceratous transformation. *Med.-News* (Philadelphia), *45*:194, 1884.

Gavan, T. L. and Kaufman, N.: Experimental renal infarction. *A. M. A. Arch. Path.*, *60*:580, 1955.

Glaister, J.: *Medical Jurisprudence and Toxicology.* Edinburgh, E. and S. Livingstone, Ltd., 1950, p. 143.

Glanville, J. N.: Postmortem serum cholesterol levels. *Brit. Med. J.*, *2*:1852, 1960.

Golin, M.: Serendipity. *J. A. M. A.*, *165*:2084, 1957.

Gossner, W.: Untersuchungen über das verhalten der phosphatasen und esterasen während per autolyse. *Virchows Arch. Path. Anat.*, *327*:304, 1955.

Graf, W.: Preserved histological structures in Egyptian mummy tissues and ancient Swedish skeletons. *Acta Anat.* (Basel), *8*:236, 1949.

Hill, E. V.: Significance of dextrose and nondextrose reducing substances in postmortem blood. *Arch. Path.*, *32*:452, 1941.

Hobson, R. P.: On an enzyme from blow-fly larvae (Lucilia sericata) which digests collagen in alkaline solution. *Biochem. J.*, *25*:1458, 1931.

Hunt, A. C.: in Camps, F. E.: *Medical and Scientific Investigations in the Christie Case.* London, Medical Publications Ltd., 1953, p. 217.

Jenkins, W. J.: The significance of blood and cerebrospinal fluid urea levels estimated after death. *J. Clin. Path.*, *6*:110, 1953.

Jennings, R. B., Kaltenbach, J. P. and Smetters, G. W.: Enzymatic changes in acute myocardial ischaemic injury. *A. M. A. Arch. Path.*, *64*:10, 1957.

Kent, S. P. and Diseker, M.: Early myocardial ischaemia. *Lab. Invest.*, *4*:398, 1955.

Kent, S. P.: Effect of postmortem autolysis on certain histochemical reactions. *A. M. A. Arch. Path.*, *64*:17, 1957.

Kernback, M., Fisi, V. and Berariu, D.: Recherches histochimiques sur les substances graisseuse pendant la putrefaction. *Ann. Méd. leg.*, *7*:598, 1927.

Kevorkian, J. and Bylsma, G. W.: Transfusion of postmortem human blood. *Am. J. Clin. Path.*, *35*(5):413, 1961.

Klauer, H. and Walcher, K.: Uber postmortale Knotchenbildung an der Haut einer Wasserleiche. *Dtsch. Z. ges. gerichtl. Med.*, *28*:464, 1937.

Krefft, S.: Zur frage der postmortalen farbveranderungen der haare. *Dtsch. Z. ges. gerichtl. Med., 44*:231, 1955.

Kühnelt, W. (I): *Soil Biology.* London, Faber & Faber, 1961, p. 243 et seq.

Ibid. (II): p. 161.

Lancet: Christmas Quiz, 2:1280, 1957.

Laves, W.: Agonal changes in blood serum. *J. Forensic Med., 7*(3):70, 1960.

Leeson, T. S.: Electron microscopy of mummified material. *Stain Technol., 34*(6):317, 1959.

Lesser, G. T., Perl, W. and Steele, J. M.: Determination of total body fat by absorption of an inert gas; measurements and results in normal human subjects. *J. Clin. Invest., 39*:1791, 1960.

Lewis, W.: On the chemical and general effects of the practice of interment in vaults and catacombs. *Lancet, 2*:125, 1851.

Libby, W. F.: Radiocarbon dating. *Science, 133*:621, 1961.

Lucas, A.: *Ancient Egyptian Materials and Industries,* 3rd edition. London, 1948.

Macleod, W.: Massacre of the Ardestine caves. *J. Roy. Army Med. Cps., 87*:10, 1946.

Mansfield, S. M.: Account of a remarkable case in which a considerable part of a female body was converted into fatty matter. *Med. and Phys. J., 3*:10, 1800.

Manson, R. T.: On the appearances presented by the bodies of 2 children exhumed at St. Helen's, Auckland. *Brit. Med. J., 11*:650, 1872.

Mant, A. K.: M. D. Thesis, University of London, 1950.

Mant, A. K.: in Simpson, C. K.: *Modern Trends in Forensic Medicine.* London, Butterworth & Co., 1953, p. 80.

Mant, A. K.: Adipocere—a review. *J. Forensic Med., 4*(1):18, 1957.

Mason, J. K., Klyne, W. and Lennox, B.: Potassium levels in the cerebrospinal fluid after death. *J. Clin. Path., 4*:231, 1951.

Mellick, R. S.: Serum-lactic dehydrogenase in diagnosis of myocardial infarction (a letter). *Lancet, 1*, 1232, 1961.

Meryman, H. T.: The mechanisms of freezing in biological systems, in Parkes, A. S.: *Recent Research in Freezing and Drying*. Oxford, Blackwell Scientific Publications, 1960, p. 23.

Middleton, J.: On the fluorine in bones, its source and its application to the determination of the geological age of fossil bones. *Proc. Geol. Soc.* (London), 4:431, 1844.

Mitchell, L. J.: Two cases of adipocere; one occurring under remarkable circumstances. *Boston Med. & Surg. J., 139*:466, 1898.

Moodie, R. L.: *Palaeopathology*. Urbana, Ill., University of Illinois Press, 1923, p. 165.

Morrione, T. G. and Mamelok, H. L.: Observations on the persistence of hepatic glycogen after death. *Am. J. Path., 28*:497, 1952.

Oakley, K. P.: The fluorine-dating method. *Yearbook Phys. Anthrop., 5*:44, 1949.

Pewe, T. L., Rivard, N. R. and Llano, G. A.: Mummified seal carcasses in the McMurdo Sound region, Antarctica. *Science, 130*:716, 1959.

Powning, R. F., Day, M. F., and Irzykiewicz, H.: Studies on the digestion of wool by insects. 2. The properties of some insect proteinases. *Aust. J. Sci. Res.* (B), 4:49, 1951.

Ramsbottom, J.: Mushrooms and Toadstools (*New Naturalist Series*), Collins, 1953.

Reay, G. A.: *Food Investigation*. Department of Scientific and Industrial Research, H. M. Stationery Office, London, 1956, p. 6.

Rosenholtz, M. and Wattenberg, L. W.: Morphologic histochemical aminopeptidase. *Arch. Path.* 71:63, 1961.

Rowling, J. T.: M. D. (Camb.) Thesis, University of Cambridge, 1960.

Rudolph, G. and Scholl, O.: Histochemische untersuchungen zum fermenthaushalt des experimentallen niereninfarktes. *Beitr. Path. Anat., 119*:13, 1958.

Ruffer, M. A.: *Studies in the Palaeopathology of Egypt*. Edited by Moodie, R. L. Univ. Chicago Press, 1921.

Sandison, A. T.: The histological examination of mummified material. *Stain. Technol., 30* (6):277, 1955.

Schleyer, F. and Janitzki, U.: Phosphate concentration in the C. S. F. and serum of dead bodies as a function of the length of time elapsed since death. *Dtsch. Z. ges gerichtl. Med.,* 49(2):229, 1959.

Schott, H. J.: The diagnosis of uraemia and of extrarenal uraemia in the cadaver with the aid of determination of rest nitrogen and urea levels in the myocardium. *Beitr. Path. Anat., 122* (1):123, 1960.

Schott, H. J.: The diagnosis of renal and extrarenal azotaemia in cadavers. *Frankfurt Z. Path., 70*(3):300, 1960.

Shaw, A. F. B.: Histological study of the mummy of Har-Mose, the singer of the 18th Dynasty. *J. Path. Bact., 47*:115, 1938.

Sinex, F. M., Faris, B.: Isolation of gelatin from ancient bones. *Science, 129*:969, 1959.

Smith, D. E., Robins, E., Eydt, K. M. and Daesch, G. E.: The validation of the quantitative histochemical method for use on postmortem material: I. The effect of time and temperature. *Lab. Invest., 6*:447, 1957.

Stewart, T. W. and Warburton, F. G.: Serum lactic dehydrogenase estimations in myocardial infarction. *Brit. Heart J., 23*(3):236, 1961.

Tolmachoff, I. P.: The carcasses of the mammoth and rhinoceros found in the frozen ground of Siberia. *Trans. Am. Phil. Soc., 23*:11, 1929.

Tripp, B. H.: Adipocere. *Boston Med. & surg. J., 10*(3):41, 1872.

Ure, A.:*Dictionary of Chemistry,* 4th ed. Tegg, T., 1831, p. 112.

van Fossan, D. D. and Clark, R. T.: Postmortem diagnosis of hypoxia by means of brain lactic acid concentration. *Am. J. Physiol., 192*:577, 1958.

van Lanker, J. L. & Holtzer, R. L.: The release of acid phosphatase and β-glucuronidase from cytoplasmic granules in the early course of autolysis, *Am. J. Path., 35*:563, 1959.

Wacker, W. E. C., and Snodgrass, P. J.: Serum LDH activity in pulmonary embolism diagnosis, *J. A. M. A., 174*:2142, 1960.

Wacker, W. E. C., Rosenthal, M., Snodgrass, P. J. and Amador, E.: Pulmonary embolism & infarction, *J. A. M. A., 178*:8, 1961.

Wagner, H. J.: Einfluss der antibiotica und sulfonamide auf die leichenfaulvis, *Dtsch. Z. ges. gerichtl. Med.*, 49:714, 1959/60.

Weiner, J. S. *and others:* Further Contributions to the Solution of the Piltdown Problem. *Bull. Brit. Mus. (Nat. Hist.)* Geology, London, 1955, vol. 2, No. 6.

Wetherill, C. M.: On adipocire and its formation. *Trans. Am. Phil. Soc., II* (new series):1, 1860.

Wilder, H. H.: The restoration of dried tissues with especial reference to human remains, *Am. Anthrop.*, 6:1, 1904.

Williams, H. U.: Gross and microscopic anatomy of two Peruvian mummies, *Arch. Path.*, 4:26, 1927.

INDEX

97